FIRST CENTURY

FIRST CENTURY

Alan Rudge

2011

FIRST CENTURY — Published by the Rev. Dr. Ashish Amos of the Indian Society for Promoting Christian Knowledge (ISPCK), Post Box 1585, 1654, Madarsa Road, Kashmere Gate, Delhi-110006.

© Author, 2011

All rights reserved. No part of this book may be reproduced or transmitted in any form or by any means, electronic, mechanical, photocopying, recording, or by any information storage and retrieval system, without the prior permission in writing from the publisher.

The views expressed in the book are those of the author and the publisher takes no responsibility for any of the statements.

ISBN: 978-81-8465-162-1

Laser typeset by
ISPCK, Post Box 1585, 1654, Madarsa Road, Kashmere Gate, Delhi-110006
• *Tel:* 23866323/22
e-mail: ashish@ispck.org.in • ella@ispck.org.in
website: www.ispck.org.in

Contents

Preface	vii
1. Early Christian Transmission	1
2. Of the Resurrection	15
3. The Christian Scene 33-43	25
4. The Facility of St. Paul's known Letters	47
5. St. Paul's Travels in 44-59	61
6. The Whereabouts of Other Prominent Christians Before 60	77
7. The Sixties	86
8. The Seventies	113
9. A Vicennium, A.D. 80 to 100	134
10. Early Second Century	153
11. Epilogue	178
Appendix Note- Mystery	190
Index	193

Preface

There is no doubt that the event of the Resurrection of Christ was followed by a period of perhaps twenty-five years of euphoria among all the people associated in the contemporary knowledge of it. Initially these were all of the Jewish culture, either as Jews nationally or as proselytes from pagan societies as "God-fearers" and they formed what Rome then, and for about a century afterwards considered to be simply another of the numerous Jewish cults not dissimilar or distinguished from the Pharisees, Sadducees, Essenes, etc; the latter two of these cults died with the Judea War of 66-70 and in the subsequent destruction of Jerusalem. The divinity and saving office of Christ Jesus because of the Resurrection were known as Nazarins, and their number probably did not exceed a few thousand by the year 38, five years after the Lord Jesus, at the time of Saul's conversion.

The disciple and Apostle John Zebedee admits in his gospel (20:8) that it was only when he had raced with Simon Peter to see the empty tomb of Jesus that he personally "first saw and believed"; he also notes that a fellow-disciple Thomas was firstly convinced of Jesus' direct connection with God the Father only in the Lord's reappearance among them after that: his honestly admitted doubt only voiced the doubt which they, as ordinary and discredited men, had all shared. St. Mark's later gospel account shows that the band of disciples did not understand what the Lord Jesus was undertaking, throughout all of His ministry among them, at the time.

The glorious Resurrection changed everything, and in this book we shall be able to look at the historical evidence available to confirm to us the fact of its history as truth, to see that it was not a charade made up as a human fiction. This is important because it revolutionized human reaction in religion, the field which deals with man's relation to God; but the central purpose of the project is to examine as far as we can the first-century link between the belief and practice held in this early euphoria and the later development and growth of an Institutional Church which might claim to be a society distinguished by the power and activity of the Holy Spirit and looking forward to the return of Christ as its Lord and Saviour to judge a world intended to be saved. The high period of linkage compassing the years 33 to about 60 is possibly the most significant era in Christian history, as coming between the time of purely Divine revelation and the rise of human interventions upon it: the literary handling by the New Testament writers between Paul and John, as a body of written witnessing, was influenced by the effect of a rising Church, but the writings did not come to be collected as a canon of books in general use until the second half of the second century.

The designation of first century here is not intended as of our Anno Domini or Jaya Christi date reckoning of years 1 to 100, which in any case is wrong with Christ now known to have been born in 8 B.C. but rather applies with the years 33 to the 130's as the century beginning with the Resurrection, the starting point of Christian belief among humanity from which it was taken up. Indications firstly from St. Mark are, that even the Lord's close followers still regarded the old Jewish hope of a political Messiah as being valid, evidenced by the fact that when He was arrested in the Garden of Gethsemane they all forsook Him and fled (Mark 14:50): they all gave up in disappointment. There is similar indication in the triumphal entry into Jerusalem described in John 12:12-19 where many seem to have felt a different euphoria in the Arrival of Their Leader, followed shortly afterwards by a vicious negative reaction in the cry "Crucify Him!" coupled with Simon Peter's denials. But, the seasons are the Lord's who sees the end from the beginning; and the Passion and Resurrection a few days later was swiftly to change everything – the greatest event in human history was not in the hands of human opinion. By the end of the century, when Polycarp was carrying the Christian torch from St. John's hands, the highly authoritative Bishop Ignatius of Antioch had been sorted out by the Romans, and the Epistle of Barnabas was written, Christendom had already changed considerably from its first days when an amazed population in Judaea rushed forward to receive baptism into the brand-new Nazarin faith. Subsequently Christianity survived down the centuries, but not in a form of the Gospel leavening the nations to bring the kingdom of God on earth; in practical development it put its trust in community leaders and manifestation through communal worship, not in the educated strength of faith in hearts and minds of the individual sheep of the community flock. For, religious education is vitally necessary for the Christian against the "catch-22" question that if people do not have faith, how are they to get it? And the acquisition of the Christian truths is an immense blessing and benefit which takes years to achieve. The survival of the Christian system as we know it has been held on worldly terms involving in the track record of history, Roman politics and Arian heresy in the fourth Century, theological confusion and schism in the fifth, Byzantine grandeur in the sixth, military adventures and worldly corruption in the medieval centuries, to arrive at irrelevance in secular societies through modernating tarnishment by the Second Millennium. Steps need to be retraced and the intervening centuries disregarded, if we would take up the torch from the second-century hands which were yet still carrying it forward, and to hold it stedfastly aloft.

> In looking far across time's ocean-wide
> Confusion of those centuries beyond
> Fire-rifted summits of the mountain range
> Behind the ruins of late Ephesus,
> To hear the voices of those former years
> And see the grand endeavour of their past
> Which links all time with its foremost event:

We are enabled, with the Christian tide,
To realize inheritance and bond
Available regardless of all change;
To build in every place, and clear of fuss,
An altar of deep peace supplanting fears,
On which to offer loyalty at last
In claim of unity which all our faith has meant.

After nineteen centuries a unity faith directly due to the marvelous blessing of Christian truth and knowledge – to make use of it – is yet awaited, always with hope. What then, might be gathered in précis as a model from that first century? The Christians then were up against difficulties in things not now seen, but fundamentals of the religious equipment new to them may be always shared. In those early days Roman opposition as such against Christianity did not loom as large as has perhaps often been thought in latter times. Nero in 64 has been involved in seizing the "followers of Chrestus" as an opportunity to ingratiate himself in his unpopularity, and at the same time find a scapegoat in the city fire at Rome; the 250-251 slavery of Decius against Christians, came much later. Jewish opposition was ever-present after about the mid-forties with Barnabas and Paul and especially along the Christian-Jew split developing in the later first century; and other opposition came from the pagans who, with Jewish accord, were behind the persecutions at Smyrna in the 150's and at Lyons in the 170's. The Christians had a valid case against paganism in so far as it was antinomian, although they did not set out to attack it on any broad front: they were concerned always with defense. The pagans generally relegated Christians on a caste basis, precluding them from numerous and particularly lucrative, occupations.

But the tenets of the faith which had lifted them out of former confusions in the secular, out of the darkness of pagan superstition, or into a new liberty of monotheistic worship beyond the blind obduracy of the erring Jews, kept them staunchly true to Christ indeed to an extent never seen in any other professed following; it is a loyalty to the true God, clean worship in the God-given liberty from falsehood. The writings of their era reflect an awareness that the Scriptures they had inherited teach morality by fundamental rules, not in specific direction to cope with every detail of possible moral doubt. The fundamental rules now in the New Testament Scriptures raised with them are rules of piety in worship (as John 4:24), of justice especially codified in the Golden Rule (Luke 6:31), of benevolence in dealing charitably (Mark 12:31 plus Luke 6:35-38), and of purity in forgiveness as the condition of receiving it from God (Mark 11:25-26). Many such examples may easily be taken from the recorded units of Christ's teaching, which generally gave effect to a practical advantage enabling greater moral certainty than was ever likely in human limitation; and they realized it. They knew that under the rule that God wills and wishes the general happiness (ref. Ezekiel 18: 20-32, Isaiah 45: 18-23, 55: 6-13, and Jeremiah 24:7) it is necessary to enquire into the tendency of actions to promote or diminish that general happiness in our given state of freewill, and to examine the designs in them. By spiritual authority as appearing at Matthew 6:5-6 and 14:23 where the gospels do not enjoin public worship for the followers of Christ but rather private devotion, private prayer in solitude which was famous among the earliest Christians revived in their minds the general impression of religious safety: it is an interview with God. Since those earliest times claim has been made in behalf of public worship that, where the greater part of mankind is unlikely to exercise any religious worship without it, a machinery for public worship is a necessary institution. However, this was not originally the formula for development of the Church; it is difficult for us far removed from them in time, to gauge the great difference which huge religious events recent with them, had made. But there is no doubt of their needing no collective structure until at least the immediate post-Resurrection euphoria had faded. In the early days the movement of the faith depended upon enlargement of the generous affections which can only come through private education, devotion, and religious realization, advantages which were firstly obtained or achieved in solitude and then expanded in lip-to-lip discussions among the yet small egalitarian groups of a kind to which Paul was invariably writing.

To some degree they are likely to have been overawed. A seriousness and sense of awe overspreads the imagination whenever the idea of the Supreme Being is meditated upon, which was new to many of the earliest Christian converts, perhaps often a majority in the small communities. In these material modern times of ours by comparison, men who see little in Christianity even supposing it to be factually true, should be reminded that as with the wisest of humankind no less, they would rejoice to find answer to their doubts and a satisfying rest to their enquiries. Times change, but people do not; and no man is a discover in proof except only that one who testified by numerous miracles that His doctrine is indeed of God. In those days before institutional church, and across the period when it was formed to be later organized, they knew that there is joy in heaven over every repentant ex-sinner, and that when the individual changes for the better the surrounding world is not itself changed one iota: the brightness is not for others. Was this possibly a seed later distorted as a "genetic modification" in the late first century Gnostic heresy? They knew that the ways of heaven are not the ways of earth, and that where there is joy in heaven over the penitence of a repentant sinner, new life is given to all that is pure and wholesome in the repentance. They needed no science for this. Kind eyes joyfully look upon the unjust steward found faithful: eyes belonging to a spirit beyond the physics of the universe and its right, constant and marvelous laws, and higher than physical life. In contrast here, our human joy is only a feeble reflection upon what our Maker is enabled, under a mechanism of freewill for the proving, at what we might do for Him. What the first century learned comes to this: that in God's intention to reconcile the individual soul-spirit to Himself, it is to become such as He was with us. Paul codified this to a degree with the formula that only Christ Jesus, believed on as God with us, can and does deliver the believer from death's law of sin; but the Christian canvas is wider that. We may learn from the first century to avoid the playing of games which make for us burdens of vain folly, in ignorance of God, which we can neither bear nor cast upon the Lord. In the universe of God's continuing creation change is the law of Nature in which He creates, dissolves, and re-creates, but principles do not change. We have long since outgrown the absurd ancient physical conceptions appearing in the Mosaic books with supposed direct Divine intervention, but we shall never out grow the genuine spiritual revelations of significance in any era.

Alan Rudge

The Original Christian Region

1
Early Christian Transmission

At the outset one must remember that the people who knew anything about the Lord Jesus resided in a fairly small geographical locality and communicated verbally: the Christian knowledge was mainly passed from lip to lip in an environment where travel was slow and not frequently undertaken by the majority. According to the evangelists Jesus had commissioned His major few followers, immediately prior to His final departure, to go outward in a purpose of teaching all nations about His achievement of embodying the salvation of humankind, a mechanism for reconciling sinning man with the holy God, a salvation available where the individual human unit itself rises to a sincere belief in this which Jesus did achieve in the general behalf. This involves all that is religiously essential, and it is likely to have formed the Creed of the believers living in that first Christian quarter-century.

The dates of writing in the Books of the New Testament canon are reasonably estimated although not known with accurate certainty, and we know that St. Luke's Acts of Apostles (i.e. some acts of some Apostles) was written in about the year 63 and thus at a time when the church was rapidly developing. Inevitably, in some aspects the development would not be necessarily wholly tuned within the uncluttered innocence which some have regarded as "primitive", a modern term applied to the church itself for the period down to as late as the fourth century conversion of Constantine when ipso facto the Church married the world. "Primary", or even "Primary Church", would be a better term against the dictionary meanings. There is a prospect that, as an example, Luke's long quotations of Simon Peter's sermon given in Acts. 2:14-35 and St. Stephen's apology in Acts. 7:2-54 may be colored by Church requirements already emerging in the early sixties – a generation after the Lord's departure – and certainly existing by the eighties. The account of the Pentecostal Visitation of Acts. 2:1-13 cannot be doubted; but there is very little scope for sufficient time in which the disciples, now only beginning to come out of their former confusion about what the Lord Jesus' ministry meant, could have formulated all of the sophisticated detailing given as associated at the time only fifty days after the Resurrection and ten days, it is believed (from Acts.1:3) after Christ's Ascension these chapters manifestly belong to a period considerably later than the days of the events they describe and of course with St. Luke, the witness is at second hand.

The earliest possibility of a Christian written form still extant with us in the Egyptian Gospel of Sayings ascribed to St. Thomas of very early date, in the original which can only be guessed at before spurious additions of Gnostic appearance were made, this document witnesses only Sayings material and nothing else; but here, notably in the Parables as presented and found also for useful comparison in the canon, there is no sign of any apparent church alignment as an organizational need. It is significant that quite frequently various points in the Egyptian Gospel appear less influenced by any later reworking, than the same or closely parallel points in Luke and Matthew. It is fair to estimate in a general way that this document is older and independent of the four evangelists of the canon, and that certain of the texts parallel with these evangelists could not be later additions by heretics who, living in later centuries, could not have thus brought them forward as their own contribution. At the time of an original writing possibly in the later thirties by St. Thomas then at Coptos in Upper Egypt, the compiler was totally convinced of Jesus as the Divine Revealer, and undertook his project to go beyond the regular oral propagation as facility to bring others to this high conviction on an individual basis: it would be available at any time for anyone to read. "Blessed are they that have not seen, and have believed" – it is a personal sharing of special knowledge at the highest level and without appeal to any further or other authority or familiarity. This purports that the writer, whoever he was, had known Jesus at first hand. The main thread of topic consists in 1. – The essential belief on Jesus as the agent of divine revelation (T1, 2, 17, 38, 75, 92, 108 and 113); 2. – Form guidance on that which a ministry should take (T14, 42, 55 and 101); and 3. – Reaction of the world to the believer (T16, 21b, 31, 58 and 68). How then, does this document "stack up" with the primal Creed of Jesus as the saving means to reconcile man with God where the holy identity of Jesus is received in true believing acceptance? To some extent the sayings character of the project, avoiding as it does any reinforcement by a use of narrative, supplies a degree of authenticity, as far as this man saw no need to illustrate and amplify, in his high endeavour. Again, at such really early date such embellishment is unlikely to have been thought of, in that a forward step from oral to papyrus was itself substantial at the time; a perceived need to add narrative details would come naturally a generation later when living memory was fading from the communities. Those parts of the Egyptian Gospel which accord as either similar or parallel with the gospels of the canon may be collected to combine in topics, and in such collection those Sayings which fall outside of any canon comparison should be rejected as probably or possibly spurious, on the reliable principle of omitting when in doubt. The collected orthodox Gospel of Sayings as ascribed to St. Thomas is then, as taken by topic, as follows:

First Topic: Direct Belief on Jesus

He who receives my words shall not taste death (T1). Let him who seeks seek until he finds; and when he finds, he shall have authority in marveling with concern (T2). In three parts of the Godhead are three manifestations united, in whom I am (T30); he who does not believe in the All – Compassing himself lacks all things (T67). I am the highest light, of the All-compassing which reached Me in the coming forth; and I am universal (T77).

Seek, and you will find. But the things you asked of Me in earlier days, I did not explain. Now that I would, you do not ask Me of those matters (T92). Yet he who seeks will find, and it will open to him (T94). He who drinks of My water will be as I am and I with him; and the hidden things will be revealed unto him (T108). The heavens and the earth will pass away, but he who lives by the Living One shall not see death (T111).

Canon References: John 11:25-26, 16:23-24, 10:30; 1 John 5:7, 5:12; John 16:23-24, 4:10; Mark 13:31.

The kingdom is within and around you. There is richness in knowledge of being sons of the Living Father, but poverty without it (T3). (The disciples asked when shall the kingdom come?) – It will come not by expectation; none may say 'Look here, or look there', but the kingdom of the Father is spread across the earth, and men do not see it (T113). (The disciples asked for analogies of the kingdom of heaven, (T51), and Jesus said,

It is like a mustard seed, smaller than all seeds. But when the seed falls on ground it puts forth a large shrub and becomes a shelter for the birds of the air (T20). The kingdom of the Father is like a merchant with goods, who found a fine pearl. Prudently he sold his goods in order to buy that single pearl. So also you must value the treasure which does not perish, and abides where no moth comes to consume it, nor worm destroy it (T77). The Kingdom of the father is like a woman who took some leaven and kneaded it in dough to raise the bread. He who has ears to hear, let him hear (T96). The kingdom is like a shepherd who had a hundred sheep. When one of these wandered away, which was the largest, leaving the ninety-nine he searched until he found that which was lost. Although tiring himself, he said 'I love this sheep more than the ninety-nine' (T107). The kingdom is like a man who had a field with a treasure hidden in it, which he knew nothing of. After his death his son inherited the field, also not aware of the treasure and the son sold it away. Then the man who had bought the field began to work it and, finding the treasure, was made glad (T109).

Behold, a sower filled his hand **with seed and sowed it**. Some, falling on a road, were gathered up by the birds. Others fell on rock where they could not make root. Others fell among thorns which choked the young seedlings and worms ate them. But others fell into good earth, raising up good fruit meet for heaven, of sixty and one hundred and twenty per measure (T9).

There was a rich man with many possessions. He said as he truly believed, 'I will use my goods to sow and reap and plant, to fill my warehouses with fruit so that I will not be in need of anything'. In that same night he died. He who has ears to hear, let him hear (Y63).

A man invited guests to a banquet, and sent his servant to them when it was ready. When the servant said 'My master requests you now' the first made excuse: 'Money is owed to me by merchants this evening, and I must deal with them; please have me excused'. Another said, 'I have bought a house, and must go to seal the contract today – there is no time'. Another said, 'I must prepare the reception dinner for my friend's wedding today, and cannot come. 'Another said, 'I have bought a farm, and must go to collect the rent there'. The servant returned to his master alone, explaining their excuses; and the master said, 'Go out into the streets and bring in those whom you most easily find, that they many partake of the feats. But the comfortable and the merchants shall not enter the places of my father (T64).

A good man who owned a vineyard rented it to tenants to work on it, as his investment. Later, he sent his servant to receive his due share from the vineyard; but they seized the servant and left him bruised. On the return of the servant to his master the master said, 'Perhaps the servant was not recognized'. He then sent another servant, but the wicked tenants beat him also. Then the master sent his son, thinking that he would be respected. But the tenant killed the son, because they knew he was the heir of the vineyard. He who has ears to hear, let him hear(T65).

The kingdom of the father is like a man who had sowed good seed, after which an enemy came by night and sowed weeds in that place also. On discovering this in the crop the farmer instructed his labourers, 'I fear that, if you pull up the weeds, you will at the same time destroy the crop. Leave alone therefore; for in the harvest time the weeds may then be surely taken out together and burned'. (T57)

Canon References: Luke 17:20-21; Mark 4:30-32; Matthew 13:45-46, 13:33; Luke 15:4-7; Matthew 13:44; Mark 4:3-9; Luke 12:16-21, 14:16-24; Mark 12:1-9; Matthew 13:24-30.

Second Topic: Guidance and Ministry

Blasphemy against the Father or the Son can be forgiven; but blasphemy against the Holy Spirit shall not be forgiven in earth or in heaven (T44).

Heaven and earth will pass away. But while you are in the light, what new thing will you do? (T11a and T11d only).

Through Me you may have what eye has not seen nor ear heard, nor any hand touched, nor the heart of man can conceive (T17). (This is quoted from Isaiah 64:4 and re-quoted by St. Paul at 1 Corinthians 2:9, but it is not recorded by the four evangelists).

(Mary asked, 'Like whom are your disciples?') – My disciples are childlike, yielding up what they have borrowed. If the owner of a house knows that a thief is coming, he will be watchful to prevent loss. Watch ye against the world, girding up your loins strongly in certain expectations. Let there be understanding among you. And when the fruit is ripe the reaper comes to reap immediately. He who has ears to hear, let him hear (T21 and T35 similar).

The babes yet unweaned are as those who enter the kingdom (T22a). There is a light within a man which may light all the world; and without it there is indeed darkness (T24). Love your brother as your own soul, keeping him as the apple of your eye (T25). Love not the world, if you would find the kingdom; and keep always the Sabbath holy and separate from all other days, or you shall not see the Father (T27).

If the blind lead the blind, both fall into a pit (T34). Take no concern through the day and night, for your apparel (T36). Do not give holy things to the dogs, for they will waste them; do not throw pearls to swine, lest they make bad of it (T93). A vine planted without the sanction of the Father is a vine that will wither and be destroyed (T40).

He who holds faithfully shall be given increase; but he with little (faith) will lose from even that little (T41). Blessed is he who has suffered, for he finds true life (T58). Blessed is the man who knows of the robbers' coming: that he may rise and gird his loins in readiness against them (T103, ref. T21). Many stand at the door, but only the elect will enter the bridal chamber (T75). Those present here who do the will of My Father, these are My brothers and sisters, and mother. These will enter the kingdom of My Father (T99).

Look to the living one in this life, lest after death you may seek Him but not find Him (T59). Come unto Me: for My yoke is easy, **My mastery is gentle,** and you will find repose (T90). I disclose my mysteries to those who are My elect. Let not your left hand know what your right hand will do (T62). The body depending on a body is wretched; and more wretched is the soul depending on flesh (T87). He who finds the world and becomes rich, let him reject (or, renounce) the world (T110).

Canon References: Mark 3: 28-29; Luke 21:33, 6:33-34, 7:31-32; Mark 13:33-37, Mark 9:36 plus Matthew 11:25; John 8:12; Mark 12:31; 1 John 2:15; Mark 2:27-28; Luke 6:25, 7:6; John 15:6; Mark 4:24-25; Luke 6:22-23; Matthew 25:1-13; Mark 3:34-35; John

7:33-34; Matthew 11:28-30, 6:3; Mark 4:11; Luke 12:4-7 and 18: 22-25.

(The disciples asked Jesus on fasting, prayer and almsgiving, also about kosher food observations): - Do not lie, nor do those things which you hate; for all things are revealed before heaven. There is nothing hidden that will not be revealed (T6). Have itinerant mobility (T42). Fasting, prayer and almsgiving are not perfection in themselves, being open to the sin of hypocrisy. In travelling through lands it is necessary that you receive that which the men of the country set before you. Heal their sick; and know that those things entering into the mouth do not defile, but that which comes out of your mouth does defile you (T14). What you hear in the ears, preach upon the housetops; for a lamp is lit not to be hidden under a measure but to be set on a lampstand to give light to all (T33).

He who cannot prefer Me above his own parents cannot be my disciple; and he who does not honour his father and mother for My sake, cannot be My disciple (T101 and T55 similar). The harvest is great, but the labourers are few. Then beseech the lord that He will send labourers into the harvest (T7).

Canon References: Luke 12:2-3; Mark 10:19, 6:7-10; Luke 6:40 plus Matthew 6:1-5; Mark 7:15-16, 4:21-23 plus Luke 12:1-3; Luke 12:1-3, Luke 14:26 plus Mark 7:10-13; Luke 10:2.

Third Topic: General and Reaction in the World

He who is near to Me is near fire; but he who is far from Me is far from the kingdom (T82). I have brought down fire, and I guard it unto its consummation (T10). I came not to bring peace to the world, but rather division. Three shall be against two in a house, two against three, the father and the son of the house in conflict, rendering them solitaries (T16). Few are chosen; but I shall choose one from a thousand, and two from ten thousand. These (elect) shall stand in a single unity (T23). But if two in a house make their peace, they may move a mountain (T43).

Appearing in the flesh I stood in the world, and saw men drunken without thirst. And My soul was pained for the sons of men who are blind of heart and who cannot see the nakedness in which they enter and leave the world. When they recover from the intoxication of material things, they will repent (T28). A prophet has no honour in his own locality; a physician cannot heal those who are over-familiar with him (T31). You do not know Me by my words to you; becoming as the people here, you either love the tree and abhor its fruit, or vice-versa (T43). Now, grapes are not gathered from thorns, nor figs from thistles – these give no fruit. Similarly a good man brings forth good from his treasure, an evil man evil from the treasure of his heart, also speaking evil. Out of the abundance of the heart comes evil (T45). Why do you wash the outside of the cup? Do you understand that the inside and outside are created together? (T89). You examine the face of the heavens and the earth, but you have not known the truth before your very eyes, nor do you know how to examine (or, appreciate) this time (T91). You see the mote in the eye of another, but not the beam in your own eye. Remove this beam, if you would have ability to clear the mote from the eye of the neighbour (T26). A city built and fortified on a high place cannot be shaken, nor hid (T32).

From Adam to John the Baptist, among those born of the flesh none is greater than John the Baptist. Yet, as I said, whoever among you becomes childlike shall know the kingdom and become greater than John (T46). Blessed are the poor, for theirs is the kingdom of heaven (T54). Blessed are ye who are hated and persecuted: for the persecutors shall find no place with you; and they whom others have persecuted in their hearts shall, the persecuted, know the Father truly (T68). Blessed are they who hunger, for they shall be filled (T69).

Woe to the Pharisees; for they are as a dog lying in the oxen's manger, which cannot eat the food of the oxen nor will allow them to eat (T102). The scribes and Pharisees took and hid the keys of knowledge. Not entering in themselves, they prevented others who would enter. Be ye then wise as serpents, and innocent as doves (T39). Did you come into the desert to see a reed shaken by the wind? Or to see a man in fine clothes? Your kings and great ones wear soft apparel, but the truth is hid from them (T78). Show Me the stone rejected by the builders; it is a cornerstone (T66).

A man cannot mount two horses nor stretch two bows. A servant cannot serve two masters, for he would then honour one and scorn the other. No man desires new wine immediately after drinking old; and one does not put new wine into old wineskins, lest they rupture, nor old into new wineskins, lest it spoil. Similarly combining old and new in patching a garment is not done, because one part would be rent (T47). Two will be seated together on a charpoy; one will die, the other live (T61a).

(One bystander asked Jesus to officiate in an inheritance):- O man, who made Me a divider? Am I a divider? (T72). Do not lend at interest, but rather give to those in need (T95). Give the things of Caesar to Caesar, and to God the things which are God's; and give what it is Mine to Me (T100). The birds have their nests, but the Son of Man has no place to lay His head and rest (T86). (A woman in the crowd remarked, 'Blessed is the womb which bore you and the breasts which fed you'):- Blessed are they who have heard the word of the Father and keep it truly. For the days will come when you will say, 'Blessed is the womb which has not conceived, and the breast which have not suckled' (T79). What sin have I committed, or by what have I been overcome? But after the bridegroom has left the bridal chamber, then let them fast and pray (T104).

Canon References: Luke 12:49-53; John 14:6-14; Mark 6:5-6; Luke 6:44-45; Matthew 23:25-26; Luke 12:54-56, 6:41-42; Matthew 5:14; Luke 7:24-28, 6:20-23, 11:52; Matthew 10:16; Luke 12:10; Mark 12:10-11; Luke 16:13; Mark 2:21-22; Luke 17:33-36, 12:13-15, 6:34-35; Mark 12:16-17 plus Matthew 20:15; Luke 9:58, 11:27-28; John 8:46; Mark 2:19-20.

The Egyptian project seems to have been assembled originally by writing the Sayings in the order of recalling them, without literary flow method, because the subjects of the Sayings are all intermixed. Within the modern exercise of editing out those parts which are outside of established orthodoxy the subjects can of course be more nearly brought together, a process which does in effect give a gospel document of really primal character, and there is no doctrinal objection *nihil obstat* in so far as the parallel canon texts furnish an authority. In this exercise we have eighty of the 114 Sayings, which is seventy per-cent; and of the thirty-four not taken up one or two may have been genuine of the lord Jesus, but none of these can be verified by checking against Other sources. Certainly there are units in the Egyptian Gospel as found in codex form in Upper Egypt which have a Gnostic appearance and were undoubtedly added at a later date, probably in the third century when the codex format of books had come into use. Beyond mere additions there is a possibility that units here were either unavailable or for some other reason unused by the four evangelists but known elsewhere, such as the note in T28 on our entering and leaving the world in nakedness, a unit which St. Barnabas may have been making direct use of in 1 Timothy 6.

In general the work strongly anticipates Christ's Sermon on the Mount as presented in the sixth of Luke, that is, without inclusion of discourse on law and the Pharisees arranged by the St. Matthew author (Matt. 5,6 and 7) for Jewish Community purposes. There are reasons for believing that the sermon was originally given privately to the newly ordained twelve disciples (vide Luke 6:12-16 with Mark 1: 35-38) but not to a crowd, and that the Lord's purpose in it immediately following His long private prayer was to give inaugural guidance of a general character to them at this earliest point of their assembled ordination – and if true, Thomas would have understood that. It means two things: 1. That the Sayings content of the Sermon forms a very basic Christian primary equipment, and 2. That only the original members of the ordained Twelve could have relayed it onwards in the detail later. Whoever was behind the Egyptian Gospel must needs be an Apostle if the date of the work is sufficiently early to be wholly independent, here assumed to be of the mid or late thirties of the first century and thus ten or fifteen years earlier than St. Paul's earliest known letter. It was not written for Gentiles; but among the diaspora of the Jews there were certainly Jews settled all along the trade route between the Mediterranean and South India to whom St. Thomas might go. If T53 is genuine it may have been known to Paul from another source; (The disciples asked Jesus about the rite of circumcision):- 'If circumcision were profitable, the Father would beget them already circumcised from their mother; but true circumcision of value is the circumcision in the Spirit'. This is not given anywhere in the canon gospel accounts, but the Hebrews author was obviously aware in a belief which this unit expresses, at Hebrews 13:9: "Be not carried about with diverse and strange doctrines. For it is a good thing that the heart be established with grace; not with meats, which have not profited them that have been occupied therein". – there seems to be no reason why this unit should be rejected out of hand as heretically spurious; and at the same time it is, again if genuine, a sharp step forward of Christian witness beyond the Jewish culture in which St. Thomas would certainly be working so early, antedating Paul.

On that important ancient trade route Upper Egypt was a remote area of settled peace in the pax Romana, and this Gospel of Sayings remained unknown outside it for centuries. Perhaps there is a clue in St. John's indication of the appellation "Thomas which is called Didymus" in John 11:16 and 20:24 in which the use of present tense is noteworthy. When John was writing, he did not say Thomas which was called Didymus, meaning "the Teacher" from the verb didow (I teach), a Greek term given at a time later than the Aramaic-speaking days when Jesus gave occasionally a nickname to an Apostle as Kephas for Simon Peter or B'ney Regesh for the Zebedee brothers. Some of the brethren at Ephesus, or their fathers, may have known of Thomas in the

[οἱ] τοῖοι οἱ λόγοι οἱ [. . . . . . οὓς ἐλά
λησεν Ἰη(σοῦ)ς ὁ ζῶν κ[ύριος ? . . . .
καὶ Θωμᾷ καὶ εἶπεν [αὐτοῖς· πᾶς ὅστις
ἂν τῶν λόγων τοῦτ[ων ἀκούσῃ θανάτου
οὐ μὴ γεύσεται. [λέγει Ἰη(σοῦ)ς·
μὴ παυσάσθω ὁ ζη[τῶν . . . . ἕως ἂν
εὕρῃ καὶ ὅταν εὕρῃ [θαμβηθήσεται καὶ θαμ
βηθεὶς βασιλεύσει κα[ὶ βασιλεύσας ἀναπα-
ήσεται.

Translation

These are the (wonderful?) words which Jesus the living (Lord) spake to . . . and Thomas, and he said unto (them), Every one that hearkens to these words shall never taste of death.

Jesus saith, Let not him who seeks . . . cease until he finds, and when he finds he shall be astonished; astonished he shall reach the kingdom, and having reached the kingdom he shall rest.

THE OXYRHYNCHUS FRAGMENT
Beginning of the Gospel of Sayings

past and elsewhere, which would explain John's expansion on this one of his fellow Apostles when he omitted even the mention of some, in his gospel as, for instance, Matthew, because there is a strong element of confirming some familiarity between Thomas and those for whom John was immediately writing. With the project of the Egyptian Gospel the environment for the single teacher coming into a remote location away from the main body of Christian circuits at an early date was certainly conducive to committing a basis of truths in written form to meet enquirers among whom, because of the isolation, a habit of oral discussion among them independently had not been formed: this was for men who were altogether outside of the post-Resurrection euphoria, in circumstance which were quite different from the later need to write narrative gospel accounts for a future beyond the witnesses' time which was felt by Simon Peter (2 Peter 1:13-14) and Barnabas (2 Timothy 4:5-8). Furthermore, illiteracy was a large factor in those days, and there is no certainty that all of the Apostles could write. As fisherman or tradesman working with their hands it was not a skill required in them, nor for centuries afterwards when literacy undoubtedly remained confined largely to Church leaders, but probably John Zebedee was always literate and Levi Matthew would have the ability to write as a tax *wallah*. What then of Thomas, in this regard? The tiny Oxyrhynchus Fragment containing Thomas 1 and 2 is too small to enable any estimate of the quality of the Greek, but on it the term kai Thoma kai eipen suggests that the given words (of Jesus the Living Lord) were "spoken again by Thomas". The oi logoi "these words" might in better Greek be rendered as logion, a collection of Sayings; it is certainly possible that St. Thomas dictated the Sayings as he recalled them, for an amanuensis to actually write down. This Fragment was discovered in the 1890's by Oxford scholars Grenfell and Hunt, but most of the document here ascribed to Thomas is recovered only from a later codex book as mere copy found in the Gnostic library at nearby Chenoboskion in 1945.

2
Of the Resurrection

Reference to Jesus the living Lord at the introduction on the Greek Fragment and the Living One in T59 reflects a probability that the Resurrection was a fact vividly forming the backdrop of the Sayings compiler's recollection and onward motive, beyond which we know in any case of factors pertaining to the historic truth of it.

In the contemporary scene of South Palestine the Pharisee sect of the Jews had believed in resurrection of the dead at some point beyond the grave or as an eventual non-visible form – of life after death as a principle. However, this was different. Nobody had come out of a tomb alive and reappeared in the flesh; and when one did so, it is likely that considerable numbers of the folk within the Pharisee following came away from it and joined the Nazarins, giving some force to the reported action of Saul of Tarsus as described in Acts. 7:57-59 and 9:1-2 in an effort to bring them back by vigorous assault on the "renegades" but not necessarily against new followers of Jesus who had not been Pharisees. Luke says at Acts. 2:41 that some three thousand souls were baptized into the Nazarin faith on a single day, which must have been occasioned by a significant event: and it is certain that the belief on Jesus was very deep indeed if the believers were willing for martyrdom as some were. Nobody would die for nothing against Nature.

Very likely in the earliest days the believers, being all Jews, were restricted in a view of Jesus ' resurrection as a miracle of God parallel to that of the raising of Lazarus which we know from the eleventh of John, and that Jesus would come again to carry out a mission of liberating first the Jews and then all mankind. The model actually in truth, that the mission of the Messiah was to die by a violent death in order to atone in the behalf of mankind for the sins of mankind, is not found in Judaism. As far as it is possible to form conclusions on this high matter the truer interpretation of Jesus' ministry and action first came into prominence with Saul's conversion experience on the Damascus road probably in the year 38, some five years after the departure of the Lord Jesus and two years after the martyrdom of St. Stephen. During the course of his religious life Saul, like Jesus in the course of His ministry, ceased to be a Jew. In that five years space between the Resurrection and the conversion of Saul the Nazarins were reflecting on what Jesus had said and done; had He simply died, full stop, they would not be doing so. They had become excited because of the new and unique phenomenon of the opened tomb and the reappearances, and of course their reflections firstly involved no written record of knowledge; their discussions consisted in personal remembrances out of which their convictions would inevitably develop over time.

By the time St. Mark came to do a written project of describing Jesus' ministry and finalizing achievement, some thirty years after Jesus which is a generation, the units of tradition in remembrance of the details had passed through numerous hands. In comparing the accounts of the three synoptic evangelists there is no surprise in finding no rigid agreement or totally concording details upon who saw the risen Jesus and identification of the places where He was seen; at their much later second-hand work done from other witness sources this is fully expected. The earliest written reference here is from Paul at 1 Corinthians 15:3-8: "The chief message I handed on to you, as it was handed on to me, was that

Christ, as the scriptures had foretold, died for our sins; that He was buried and then, as the Scriptures had foretold, rose again on the third day. That He was seen by Cephas (i.e. Simon Peter), then by the eleven Apostles, and afterwards by more than five hundred of the brethren at once, most of whom are alive at this day, though some have gone to their rest. Then He was seen by James, then by all the Apostles. "This gives five separate and distinct appearances, written of in about the year 54, and Paul's note "And last of all I also saw Him, as one born out of due time" undoubtedly refers to spiritual sight in the vision graciously vouchsafed to him on the open road. This was a different experience than had been the regular physical presence with the main body of Apostles five years earlier and twenty-one years before the writing of this letter.

"As the Scriptures had foretold, died for our sins". Here is a sudden leap forward within the era of post-Resurrection euphoria, an early evidence of the connecting of the Christian events back to the Classical Prophets: a faith system which differed from all other religious followings in that it centred in a historical figure of Jesus, of one substance with God, becoming man to suffer on the cross and was resurrected according to the Scriptures. It contrasted with all existing philosophies. The fact of there being a substantial body of Nazarins in convinced belief at the time does indicate that, even if their collective interpretation of what the Resurrection meant was not yet agreed in all details within its scope, the main outlines of their unity of faith were sufficiently established to be already a force to reckon with. These aspects were brought to a wide and permanent form when St. Mark wrote his gospel in the sixties, but at only one verse (Mark 15:28) does he directly note "And the Scriptures was fulfilled". At several other points, viz. Mark 8:31, 9:31, 10:33-34, 12:10-11 and 14:27-28 specific occasions for prophetic references were open, but none were made. On the whole Mark was still showing Jesus as the great and unique teaching rabbi, as understood by those around

Him before the Resurrection, writing within the context of the time of that teaching. But in their contemporary life all the evangelists took, as did the writer of the Egyptian Gospel, the divinity, authority and power of Jesus, for granted after His reappearances.

There is no means of knowing how far the believers in the period between 33 and 41, when Saul came into circulation after being minted and polished, so to speak (three years of delay, according to his note at Galatians 1:17-18) used this scriptural credal formula; but it is fairly certain that various traditions existed in regard to making interpretation from the known details of the Resurrection during that fairly long period of eight years, and quite definite that their faith in it remained bright. The event of the Resurrection over which they took some time to come to terms was never a matter for argument, and the Gospel of Sayings seems to testify to a contemporary belief firstly that in this high event God witnessed to His Son, whatever may have been their ideas about the office of the Messiah. The contrast between the inevitably Jewish outlook at the very beginning and the new basis of the Resurrection as the central Christian hope to which 1 Peter 1:3 refers, appears to arise with Paul as well seen in 1 Corinthians 15:12-20 – if Christ were not risen we would be guilty of giving false testimony, your faith would be a delusion and you would be stuck forever in the consequences of your sins. But in truth Christ has risen from the dead, the first fruit of all when they have entered the sleep of death. The question in this from the point of view of dating is, how soon might Paul have formulated his excellent leavening of the faith system apparatus after his conversion? As Saul the zealous Pharisee the effort to get himself right with God by the means of mere adherence to Jewish Law almost finished him (Galatians 3:21), and the experience in sudden realization of where he had been wrong in attempting the impossible had the effect of bringing him violently to the truth. Probably as an educated Pharisee he saw the scriptural prophecies behind Jesus suddenly from that road experience which he described (Acts 26:12-18) to Agrippa, and this constituted his own personal conversion with utter conviction. In this hypothesis one may remember that as a Hellenistic Jew in cosmopolitan circumstances he had advantages which Jews in general have never possessed.

Saul was in Jerusalem in early Christian years, as for instance when Stephen was martyred; but in all probability he heard of Jesus only through the fact of the many conversions there, since it is unlikely that he could have moved against the Nazarins if he had earlier known of the Resurrection event at first hand. Had he been present at the time, what might he have concluded in the evidence of it before his very eyes? In the immense leisure of hindsight we can examine the evidence ourselves to see firstly that the friendly involvement of two fellow Pharisees Joseph of Arimathea and Nicodemus in the burial of this man whom the rival and opposing sect of Sadducees had dragged to His death, made the burial. There could be no doubt that Jesus was physically dead when the Roman authority released the body to Joseph and that even if still alive, the entombed man could not escape from the heavily enclosed tomb. Given their fear of Jesus indicated at John 11:45-53 the Sadducee priestly interest would almost certainly be watching against any attempt by others to remove the corpse from the tomb; indeed, Matthew 27:32-66 says they did, as also did a letter which I will show you in a moment. Certainly not undertaking it themselves, they may have actually hoped to find someone else doing it, which would expose an imposture and reinforce their position of pretending that Jesus was fake. No candidate appears for a project of stealing the corpse, because further it is certain that the disciples of Jesus were lying low in the hostile circumstances about which they had been able to do nothing. John 20:19a says that they had locked their door "for fear of the Jews", by Mark 14:50 they had all forsaken Jesus and fled from the scene of arrest; they were now in a state of unbelief as well as shock. The removal of the stone closing the tomb of typical contemporary Palestine design would require a heavy gang of six to accomplish it, but in any case the management of the corpse by the two Pharisees who had been impressed by Jesus took matters out of the hands of the disciples, and neither of these men would be likely to play any further game after they had carefully supervised the burial according to their cultural requirements. It is irritating that the final part of the original St. Mark scroll, in which post-Resurrection details would have been well described, was broken off and lost, but the St. Matthew author at Matthew 27: 62-66, 28: 4b and 28:11-15 gives a note of a guard mounted at the tomb. It is likely because, since an interference with the corpse might result in a riot to be not a Jewish but a Roman peacekeeping problem, Roman interest was possible in mounting a guard over this burial of unusually a Jewish working-class freeman in a wealthy tomb, at least as great as any Sadducee interest. There was not likely to be any difficulty in persuading Pilate to furnish it. In the Roman system such guard consisted of sixteen men who, if they failed in the duty, would be under sentence of execution. A seal consisting of a rope stretched over the closing stone and fastened at each end with a sealing device, was applied. In particular the application of the Roman koustodia takes this matter beyond human hands and into the prospect of supernatural action in the opening of the tomb, because the guard under severe military order would have prevented it under the burden of duty, had they been able.

The fate of the guardsmen is not of interest, but the St. Matthew author notes that they reported not to the army but to the priests from whom they received bribe money to lie about the event of the opening. This seems to have got back to Pontius Pilate, whose view included a preference to have good relations with the local Jewish leaders as far as possible within the Roman duty of keeping the peace and administration. A letter purporting to be written to Claudius (not to the current emperor Tiberius who gave short shrift to officers deemed to waver) is traceable from Tertullian (Apoligeticus 5:21) late second century in the west, which supports Matthew:

"Pontio Pilato to Claudius, Greeting.

I was recently concerned in a strange occurrence. The Jews in this place, through envy, took vengeance upon one of themselves, a Rabbi with particular claims who was variously seen to perform healing miracles, to exorcise demons, and to raise the dead. The main body of their priests then caused him to be brought before me, with the accusation that he was worthy of death, as being a sorcerer who had broken their law.

Believing this, I ordered a flagellation and delivered him to their desire to have him crucified. They requested a guard over the tomb of this man; but while my soldiers maintained this guard, he arose. Fearful in their wickedness the Jews paid over money to the soldiers as an inducement that they should make report to the effect that the corpse had been stolen away by the followers of him.

Although they took this bribe, the soldiers did not remain silent. Reporting a rising from this tomb, they revealed the Jewish payment. Because of this, I have reported the case to you, against the chance that more may come of it, with false versions, to Rome".

There being no reason against it, this letter is assumed genuine; and if genuine, Pilate seems to have been sure that the opening of the tomb was an action his guard could not handle. Besides these factors evidence, a plot to foster belief probably would have resulted in a more coherent story than that which assembles from the four evangelists, but in any case the believers were people of high moral integrity unlikely to base a belief on fiction. Moreover, there were many still living for years who could refute anything historically untrue: nobody could get away with making it all up. Again, any interest seeking to put a stop to the reported surge of belief after the discovery of the open and empty tomb could soon do so by producing the dead body of Christ, but none could. There was no longer a Corpus Christi. Nor could Paul invent a record of Jesus being seen afterwards, whether he had been in Jerusalem in 33 or not, a group of reappearances variously described alter by all four evangelists whose sources varied. St. John, the only eyewitness among them, was concerned at the personal level with specific individuals in these reappearances, especially with Mary Magdalene whom Jesus quickly rescued from the brink of a nervous breakdown (John 20:11 and 20:15-17), and Thomas whom he elaborated deliberately for his readers (John 20: 27-29). Christ's purpose in reappearing was, to give forward motion to His followers for a ministry into the future regarding Himself, and it changed their lives. Their unbelieving sorrow at the loss of a friend was elevated to an enthusiasm for ministry in the service of the conqueror of death, an enthusiasm which would a few years later be further elevated in the ministry of St. Paul. We only occasionally realize that God delays His aiding purpose where, had His blessing come sooner; its full fruit would have been missed. Had Paul been present among them at the outset, his level of belief might have been limited to much less than it ultimately was. By the later revelation enabling him to tie back to the Resurrection and his religious education keeping him mindful of the ancient prophets, the fruit of faith was brought to the full.

In viewing the important fact of the unique Resurrection some attention should be given to the subject in terms of theological belief. Doctrines – as either of a common eschatological event beyond earth or as an individual soul experience – date back to earliest times of religious adherence in various cultures. Such belief did not begin with the ministry of Jesus which founded Christianity, but was irrefutably confirmed by it. The visible historical difference made by this confirmation is that by it the Christian believers were guaranteed in the efficacy of their faith to all degrees, to the extent of martyrdom under persecution. In the ancient monotheistic faith of the Hebrews a practical and forward belief in resurrection is remarkably absent, certainly before the sixth century B.C. time of the Captivity of them, being referred only in Daniel 12: 1-2 of early second century B.C. date, where the Archangel Michael is said to act, "Many of them that sleep in the dust of the earth shall awake, some to everlasting life, and others to shame and everlasting contempt". Daniel may be fairly regarded as an apocryphal book, but this text was almost certainly a basis of resurrectional belief among the Jewish sect of the Pharisees which dated from about 150 B.C. in its origin, and it may have been lifted from Persian beliefs further east. Where Job 19:25-27 (the oldest book of the Old Testament c. 1500 B.C.) expresses a belief in seeing our Redeemer, it was a desperate cry from the heart in hope that it would be so, rather than a confident statement; in the literal construing, "If only I knew that this must be true". There were muddled beliefs entrenched in human self-interest both before the event of the Resurrection, in pagan ideas and later Jewish writings involving exclusion of those denying their authority, and after it in Mediterranean churches assuming a necessity to be baptized within them to secure salvation. For the Christian the whole matter is expressed with the utmost clarity by Christ's words relayed by the reliable witnessing of St. John in his narrative about the raising of Lazarus (John 11: 25-26) certainly applicable to the individual believer, regardless of all else: "I am the resurrection and the life. He that believeth in Me, though he were dead, yet shall he live; and whosoever liveth and believeth in Me shall never die". All you need is faith in God, remembering that whatever formulae may be dreamed up by collective interests whether pagan, Jewish, or Church, it remains true that one on God's side is a majority.

As a unique and supernatural event the resurrection of Christ Jesus the Messiah was a visible signature upon just that above-quoted text of John, in circumstances of Divine ordinance in which human knowledge of the hereafter is not legal here below: it is not for us to know anything of what is beyond the grave which terminates the sinning state for the individual leaving it behind. There is nothing available to convince in argument through reason – faith transcends reason. The historical event here gives a particular ground of hope of participation with Christ (vide 1 Peter 1:3-5, carried forward by 3:14-15 ibid). Deriving directly from Christ's demonstration, without any notion of our being resurrected here in the flesh as He was. Certainly St. Paul based his theology in this hope, expressed especially at 1 Corinthians 15:22 "As in Adam all die, even so in Christ shall all be made alive", beyond which certainty he made personal guesses, but we can be sure that in an individual resurrection which implies restoration and renovation of the believer beyond the Father's season of earth life for him, there will be implementation of a necessary sea-change. In fine, in belonging to Christ through the sincere holding of faith in Him the believing human unit shares in His resurrection by a certainty conferred by His physical demonstration of raising to life by the power of God, and the change is already initiated by the new heart attained by one who chooses Christ as the basis of this limited life and to the best possible extents rejects all else. Here the Agent of the change is the Holy Spirit at work in the body unit; Paul's idea of resurrection of the body (1 Cor. 15:38-44) can only be sustained on this basis. The theologically important point is that, whatever may happen to the body vehicle, that conjoined in it will, as a new man already in Christ, be received resurrected into reappearance to participate in His messianic victory. The very earliest Christians beyond Christ's Ascension (including persons who had not seen Him equally with those who had) were no longer left in the realms of fantasy, but were sustained by the transforming experience of knowing that the living Christ had demonstrated His highest claims by means of that physical and supernatural phenomenon designed for their facility. In this, the New Testament evidence was preserved so that in all ages we any sustained in it likewise. Glory to God in the highest.

3
The Christian Scene 33-43

Historically this period may be regarded as the first Christian epoch. From the beginning, the point in time when the Lord Jesus appeared again as having risen from the death tomb, there was never any distinction between the Jesus of history and the Christ of faith. Such miracles of the supernatural had never before been seen, and in a real sense this which gave rise to faith for the contemporaries simultaneously gave the guarantee of Jesus as the historical figure par excellence, one individual whose sojourn in the world has had immeasurable impact far exceeding any other in either depth or perpetuity of it. The earliest believers could not be aware of these aspects since, apart from the need for time in which the historical significance would develop, their capacity to express the newly rising religious faith could come only gradually, perhaps requiring several years spent in discussion across the backcloth of Jesus personally remembered. In the important matter of the reappearances it seems that no consensus had been reached among the traditional units of witness; not only are the evangelists not consistent here (vide "Mark" 16: 9-14) – but this was a later addition), John 20: 14-29 most reliably, Luke 24: 15-51 and Matthew 28: 9-20), but St. Paul in 1 Corinthians 15: 40-53 seems to have felt a lack of words to describe the risen Jesus purely in terms of the flesh. They had the historical facts, Jesus was not seen as a ghost or as a resuscitated corpse; but clearly they had doctrinal difficulties in accommodating a satisfactory understanding of the physical part of the miracle into their infant state of faith. Luke traveled substantially with Paul, and it is probable that he was still seeking to deal with this conundrum when he wrote his collected gospel account in about the year 80, the detail particularly visible with him at Luke 24: 38-39 "and He said uto them, Why are ye troubled? And why do thoughts arise in our hearts? Behold, my hands and My feet, that it is I Myself: handle Me, and see; for a spirit hath not flesh and bones, as ye see Me have". Jesus then had something to eat, by which the record of physical reality is completed. The Christian system is manifest in that a new human unit, whole and regenerated in body, soul and mind, is possible in redemption, and this has a corporeal component based on incarnation eventually expressed in resurrection. However, this clarity of doctrinal accommodation with the certain historical facts came only slowly, requiring most of the first century for its final arrival at formulation. Near the end of the century St. John also picked up this topic of spiritual faith on the one hand and flesh and blood on the other, as at John 12: 14; "And the Word was made flesh, and dwelt among us; and we beheld His glory, the glory as of the only begotten (or, one of a kind) of the Father, full of grace and truth". In 1 John 5: 4-9 containing testimony to Trinitarian belief, "Spirit, water and blood: these three (also) agree in one". As with the Nicodemus interview in John 3 we ought to construe the term "born again" or "born of God" as begotten; indeed, the entire general Epistle First John is a concern of the believer divinely rebegotten. In this project St. John evidently saw a late-century contemporary need to stress it, but this may also involve some degree of remembering the early days and a particular pleasure in pointing back to them.

By using John 19:31 together with the metonic nineteen-year cycles (each containing seven leap years) of the Jewish calendar and making associated calculations of lunation's, it is possible to arrive at the crucifixion date as 9 April 33 which sets the Resurrection at 12 April, Christi's Ascension 26 May, and Pentecost

5 June that year. For some time after that, according to Acts. The believers were all at Jerusalem, meeting in fellowship with the Eucharist and prayers and holding community of property (Acts 2: 42-45) on the principle "From each according to ability, to each according to need" (Acts 4: 32-35). The Christian population at that time was perhaps just over three thousand. The narrative continues with Simon Peter and John working together in Jerusalem in an outreach claiming to continue the healing miracles of Jesus and involving teaching and preaching, all entirely within the Jewish cultural ethos. In the course of this they were arrested and brought before a Sanhedrim Council to that which had "tried" Jesus. The priestly names given at Acts 4:6 indicated that at least one year had elapsed between these trials; the Caiaphas of John 11:49 "being the high priest that year" appears in the trial of the Apostles, but no longer in the high office. The new high priest named as Annas did not suffer from the jitters as had Caiaphas earlier regarding Jesus, so the Apostles were only ineffectually threatened against further Christian outreach, a threat which was totally ignored. The author Luke then reverts to a brief continuance about the Church as a communion of believing brethren, mentioning the Cyprus Levite Joses, renamed here by the Apostles as Bar Nabas "Son of Encouragement" who sold himself up and gave the proceeds to the church. All this seems to have occurred in the year 34, this part of the narration ending with further friction with the Sadducean priests with a short imprisonment from which the Apostles either escaped or were released. Clearly the matter of the Apostles teaching and working in Jerusalem as representing Christ had got beyond the capacity of the established vested interests to handle it in opposition. By Acts 5:26 "Then went the captain with the officers, and brought them (i.e. the Apostles) without violence: for they feared the people, lest they should have been stoned". One member of the Council of priests named Gamaliel gave a sensible summing-up of the situation as something against which they could not ultimately fight; it is uncertain as to whether this is identical with the

Gamaliel of Acts 22:3 under whom Saul originally studied as a Pharisee student at either Jerusalem or Tarsus, but probably it was one and the same. The portion Acts 6: 1-7 is likely to embrace all of the year 35, brief though it is. In the following year Pontius Pilate's tour of duty as procurator (known to be 26-36) ended, and immediately in his absence it was possible for Jewish anti-Nazarin interests to lynch St. Stephen Josephus describes a tumult in Samaria resulting in Pilate's recall to Rome: " But when this tumult was appeased, the Samaritan Senate sent an embassy to Vitellius, president of Syria, and accused Pilate of the murder of those who were killed; for that they did not go to Tiranthaba in order to revolt from the Romans, but to escape the violence of Pilate. So Vitellius sent Marcellus, a friend to answer before the emperor to the accusation of the Jews". (Antiquities of the Jews" Book 18.4.1 and 2). No time space between Pilate and Marcellus is indicated, but even one day in between would be sufficient to enable the lawless lynching. It is at this point in time in the year 36[*] that we first meet Saul of Tarsus (Acts 7:58 and 8: 1-3) and owing to rapid growth of a persecution against the Nazarins only the Apostles remained in Jerusalem, other believers now being scattered abroad as a kind of Christian diaspora.

Among the apostles here in the mid-thirties Philip is known to have spent more time in Samaria with a good deal of success, from which Simon Peter and John followed suit, preaching the Gospel in many Samaritan villages (Acts 8: 25), while Philip then traveled south to Gaza and then up the Palestine coast to Caesarea (verse 40 ibid). Simon Peter and John returned to Jerusalem to stay some time there; but from what Paul says in Galatians 1: 18-19 John was no longer there in 41, only James the head of the Jewish Church, with Simon Peter also noted there at the time. There is considerable probability that John went back to Samaria,

---

[*] or Early 37; Josephus – "Before Pilate could get to Rome, Tiberius was dead". This Emperor died 16 March 37 and Stephen's Martyrdom was perhaps in January of that year.

a land where his gospel shows some affection. Thomas appears likely in Upper Egypt, beyond which he possibly traveled onward to meet enquiries from Jews settled in Kerala at the southern end of the Graeco-Roman trade route. Philip appears as the diplomat of the apostolate (John 12:20-22 and 14: 8-9), and his pioneer action firstly in Samaria was repeated at Caesarea, to which district Simon Peter again followed later (Acts 9:32; 10:48). Regularly only this little amount is known of the Apostles early travels.

In compiling the necessary draft for his book Acts of Apostles Luke appears to have depended on two main sources, chronologically reversed. Firstly, St. Paul with whom he traveled for some considerable time if we may directly regard the abrupt switch of the writer from third to first person plural, "they" to "we" at Acts 16: 8-10, thereafter remaining in that later used part of speech, and secondly someone at Jerusalem around the year 59, very likely St. James, as a necessary source for the first section of the record Chapters 1 to 12 inclusive. James could have relayed the main lines of Simon Peter's speeches in this section as for instance given at Acts 2: 22-24 plus 2: 32-36 and his accommodation of the Gentiles as something new, in Acts 10:26-48, similarly the doctrinal units of Christ's sermon on the Mount for Luke 6: 20-23 and 6: 27-49, because this leader of the Jerusalem Church was almost certainly present throughout, and was still alive there when Paul (and, by the close and substantial details of the voyage to Rome, Luke as well) departed for Rome near the turn of the year 59-60; it was a two years period 57-59 when Paul was held at Jerusalem in Roman custody.

In the days before the coming of Paul, a period in which the record of Simon Peter's reported units of faith belief applies, these units were assembled into a faith equipment embracing a hope based in the Resurrection of the crucified Christ, with the model that all may, by repentance and baptism, receive the gift of the Holy Ghost. It was put directly into practice at Caesarea (Acts 10: 45-48) in 40 or early 41, forming the earliest record not only of outreach to the Gentiles but also of an interpretation from the Resurrection that our salvation is secured by a repentant and sincere belief on the name of Christ Jesus as the given means of salvation. In the second of Acts Simon Peter's faith witness back in 33 is confined to Jesus raised up as the Jewish Messiah: for at least the first five or six years probably the Nazarins still believed Jesus, as their Messiah, to be just the anciently anticipated saving politician of their nation "according to the Scriptures", as with the references to David in Acts 2 in a prospect of "letting all the House of Israel know". In the earliest stage they were unaware of the Divine universality, yet in the St. Thomas Egyptian Gospel none of this is stressed, nor attention drawn to it – although certainly it was a Jewish document. The Sayings collection furnished a manual for right living based on the Rock of Jesus by following what He taught, as far as the document goes. Of course no indication towards Gentile accommodation is to be expected at its similarly early date, when the interpretation thus far consisted in absorbing the light of teaching newly vouchsafed by Jesus denoted as the Living One, from and within the excitement of the aftermath of His Resurrection, unto a new life.

The Arrival of Saul among the Apostles initiates the second phase of this early Christian epoch. As far as can be estimated the state of faith belief with the Nazarins in about the year 40 encompassed a knowledge of Jesus' ministry in which its terminating events had abruptly caused them to "sit up and take notice", resulting in an assembling of some of His precepts seeming to the compiler to be the most significant as seen at the time, and then a development at the end of the thirties decade of salvation in reconciliation of repentant and believing mankind to God through accepting Christ Jesus the saving Son. As far as the limited record shows, this development was largely owing to Simon Peter through his particular work along the Palestine coast, where he applied the principle of the Holy Ghost granted universally. Before this, there appears to have been a preoccupation with their Jewish roots expressed as of the holy vine of David, this still visible with

St. Stephen in the narrative of Acts 7. It is difficult to find specific identification of the Lord Jesus primarily as the universally saving Christ in the thirties; and with Simon Peter at Acts 2:23 for instance the testimony is limited indeed, to men slaying Christ whom God raised up. But in the field of Church the bringing of material things into common ownership and the appointing of deacons for the management of benefits points to an early establishing of Christian conscience along the practical lines of following the Lord's example and teaching, veering away now from the Jewish world in this; there was practicality in the Christian system earlier than a full doctrinal realization. As yet, there was no conflict between Gentile and Jewish Christians, but discord between divergent Jewish Christians is possible in the period when Stephen was martyred; Stephen did not really address the charges brought against him – his defense was confined to giving an apologia of Old Testament material. Very likely the martyrdom of Stephen marks the point in time where the Nazarins ceased to use the Jerusalem temple as a place of worship, and also the starting point for Christian re-interpretation of the religious law as the law fulfilled in Christ. It is into this general faith environment that Saul of Tarsus came, in the three years following his remarkable conversion while on a journey to Damascus. The major current prospect was this: that until Barnabas and Saul arrived; the Nazarin believers did not so far absorb the significance of the prophetic Messianic Texts in the office and work of the Lord Jesus. Possibly the Apostles were not well versed in the Classical Prophets; and the gospel accounts do not indicate Jesus ever giving them any master-class in this field. Where Luke 24:25 says that the Lord upbraided two followers for their ignorance of the Scriptures, the text here appears to be spurious, because the idea of His acting out a charade of a stranger speaking in this way alien to all we know of His methods, and in the course of one of His reappearances, is not tenable. More likely it is, that He did appear for them as they were in every sense walking away, with the result that they returned immediately with delight to Jerusalem to rejoin the others: nothing else.

With the fact of his nephew Mark (Colossians 4:10) living at Jerusalem (Acts 12:12), Barnabas in Cyprus (Acts 4: 36) is likely to have received news of the Resurrection quite quickly, and from a journey which even in those days would have taken only a week or ten days, it is easily possible that he was present at the Pentecost when the Apostles were, by unction of the Holy Spirit, given gifts of utterance. Undoubtedly it was a divine ordinance that the believers would have a period of several years supplying an intervening space between the opportunity of the Jews and the onward provision of it to the Gentiles. And surely also Saul of Tarsus, originally walking in deep error but having great potential for regeneration was a chosen vessel of the Lord, as thereby manifest as the powerful instrument of conversion brought supernaturally upon him: "I am Jesus, whom you are persecuting". The text at Acts 9:20 says that he preached the truth at Damascus in a synagogue of the Jews that Christ is the son of God, a title offensive to the Jews there as elsewhere, and in verse 22 ibid that he offered proofs of it, which could only be done by using the Scriptures. Some time later, after escaping from an attempt on his life, Saul came to Jerusalem and apparently at this time met Barnabas, who introduced him to the main body of believers; but here Luke notes that the Apostles organized his return to his home town of Tarsus, and this would be in the year 40. In Galatians 1: 11-16 he confirms the revelation of Christ Jesus as the Son of God to be the formula for his preaching, displacing "the traditions of my fathers... in the Jews religion". But then he discounts Jerusalem at the time, saying that he went there after a lapse of three years spent in Arabia and at Damascus. This record is somewhat garbled, with little occasion for him to go again to Damascus after his serious escape, but the noted three years gap down to Jerusalem is virtually certain. By this time, in 41 Simon Peter had initiated the possibility of embracing Gentiles in the new faith system, and Acts 11: 19-22 describes a substantial outreach along the north-east corner of the Mediterranean. Barnabas then went to Tarsus to get Saul, to whom in all probability he was attracted by Saul's scriptural commitment in taking up the Nazarin faith. As a Levite Barnabas would be similarly educated, so these men were able to become a working unit in the year they now spent at Antioch (Acts 11:26) when and where the believers came to be known as Christians. In the chronology Acts 12 really belongs between chapters 15 and 16. The great significance of these secondary and educated Apostles appears at Acts. 13:2 in the divine unction: "Separate Me Barnabas and Saul for the work whereunto I have called them". In the narrative where Luke notes that here the believers were first called Christians, the style of this appellation may have been originated by outsiders rather than by the brethren themselves; and a time span appears with this part of the text in that at Acts 11:27-28 a prophecy of future famine by one Agabus is also noted, as future to this the year 41. The date of the famine which did occur is known to be the year 46 which indeed was in the reign of Claudius Caesar (41-54).

The arrival of St. Barnabas, known always by this name given to him by the original Apostles, can to some extent be visualized with a secular parallel. Suppose a member of parliament to have a sister's family living in the capital of another State not very far distant where a sudden great occurrence of hope had brought thousands of the lower castes into a new movement which his own political experience and belief told him was essentially right. This brings him quickly to the city where he remains, notwithstanding local opposition by the long-established politicians in that place, who fear a revolution to the extent that they arrest and kill some of the newly dissenting people during the next few years; this whole experience convinces him in the new movement, and henceforward he elects to serve it, putting his skills and experience at its disposal as signaled practically by selling himself up and giving the proceeds to the party. This was in principle the position of Barnabas with the Nazarins in their religious movement at Jerusalem. From the moment of the discovered opened and empty tomb of Christ they had all realized the glorious Resurrection to be an Act of God, but this man is the earliest in the movement with whom a literal linking of Jesus back to the ancient prophecies concerning the whole matter is certain, antedating the same linking by St. Paul whom Barnabas befriended when others did not. This friendship was instrumental in bringing Saul, or Paul, early into the Christian mainstream, whatever had been his zeal at Damascus. However, in Galatians 1:11-24 Paul does not give Barnabas the credit of it where it was due, saying only at 2:1 ibid that he was accompanied by Barnabas on a later visit to Jerusalem. Here the quoted fourteen years does not work in Luke's chronology: the Jerusalem conference on circumcision was in 54, ten years after the first tour. At Corinthians 11: 32-33 Paul refers to his difficulty at Damascus where a vassal king Aretas IV controlled the city and thus the many Jews living there were not closely under the regular Roman peacekeeping. From Acts 9:26-27 clearly Barnabas was in Jerusalem when Saul came there from Damascus, but the record gives no specific information about them necessarily meeting either there or earlier, before Barnabas introduced Saul to the brethren; and Saul now being sent home to Tarsus suggests that the brethren remained unsatisfied in their apprehension of him (Acts 9:26). The next note of them concerned the bringing of Saul back not to Jerusalem but to Antioch (Acts 11: 22-30) where Barnabas, described as "a good man, and full of the Holy Ghost and of faith" was sent from Jerusalem seemingly as a community leader at Antioch "exhorting them all" there.

According to Acts 11: 19-21 there was in the period 36-41 a substantial outreach of missionary work – but only to Jews – as far a field as Cyprus but evidently based at Antioch, which arose from believers scattering away from the difficult environment of Jerusalem. Luke notes here that this was the reason for Barnabas being sent to that rising Christian centre as a city of some importance in secular. Antioch in Syria was then the third city of the Roman Empire after Rome and Alexandria, a Hellenistic city with a cosmopolitan population enjoying material prosperity where Greek civilization flourished in contact with Oriental culture. Initially the Christian outreach would inevitably be to the large Jewish community there, but the pax Romana of the Roman system gave a good degree of security unavailable at Jerusalem. There are indications of an electic intellectual spirit of religious enquiry existing at Antioch, in which Greek-speaking Jews who were fugitives from Jerusalem in the mid-thirties could offer preaching activities particularly to Jew proselytes and Greek-speaking Gentiles. By Acts 11:21 many were converted here, even before the arrival of some Apostles: it was a location promising good prospects. After spending a year in the city Barnabas and Saul took a collect to Jerusalem and soon returned (acts 11:25-30 and 12:25), bringing John Mark with them while undoubtedly realizing that Antioch was fast displacing Jerusalem as the major current Christian centre. The narrative in the Book of Acts now enters upon the important topic of the first missionary outreach to other lands, started by the appointing of Barnabas and Saul to this work; they appear to have embarked without delay, taking John Mark with them for assisting work in the ministry, sailing from Seleucia which was the port for Antioch, to Cyprus. It is likely that the environment from which they set out was one of small mixed communities with the Acts 13:1, meeting for fellowship, learning, eucharist and prayer in private houses as they were still doing in the fifties at Corinth (1 Corinthians 16:19). Certainly the Apostles and Mark received a community blessing when they were sent forth by the Holy Ghost (Acts 13:3-4).

Barnabas had been living in Cyprus when functioning as a Levite, and it seems significant that this country was chosen as the direction of their travel rather than Saul's home town of Tarsus involving about the same geographical distance but requiring a sea voyage in competition with a route along good Roman roads between Antioch and Tarsus. The point of their arrival is indicated as Salamis in south-east Cyprus, from which after a short stay they traveled along the south side of the island to the port of Paphos in the south-west. This place was the Roman capital of Cyprus, itself a senatorial province from 22 B.C. where the governor had the title of proconsul. At Salamis they had preached in the Synagogue of the Jews; so evidently a sentence of excommunication published against confession that Jesus is the Christ, at Jerusalem, was not in force in Cyprus if as it seems from Acts 13:55 they were not thrown out of the synagogue here. At Paphos they met their first difficulty. Probably Barnabas knew this city that it was celebrated by a temple there dedicated to Venus, essentially a pagan centre of infamous licentiousness of practices, but it was new to Saul. In the account of some business with a local sorcerer in Acts 13: 6-12 this man, named as Elymas, was interested in preventing any success of the Apostles in an interview with the deputy governor Sergius Paulus who had required their attendance. It is at this point in the narrative that Luke says Saul adopted a new name of Paul (Latin "small one") which may be a remarkable coincidence but seems more likely to be adopted from the deputy. Elymas saw that his influence previously enjoyed in the city was about to be supplanted, and actively interfered with the Apostles giving their message to the interested official. But the next verses Acts 13: 9-11 need to be read carefully, remembering that Paul was almost certainly Luke's source in this portion. It is unlikely that "the hand of the Lord was on Elymas" upon a direction from Paul; in much plainer language Paul hit him in the face. In any event the deputy was impressed by the vigor of the reaction, but such action would leave Barnabas and especially Mark singularly unimpressed: Christians do not manage a matter by losing their temper and using their fists. It is important to consider that Paul was as yet only recently become a Christian, and the zeal he had been accustomed to apply in his earlier Pharisee dealings was still with him. If his known letters are arranged in chronological order it is possible to see that he did successfully "put off the old man" over time; there is a wide personal difference between the letter to the Galatians with "O foolish Galatians, who hath bewitched you?" and that to his beloved Philippians. St. Paul's conviction and strength of faith in Christ was truly excellent from the day of his conversion, but personally and on the secular side he seems to have had few staunch friends and perhaps was not in general best of companions. The narrative given in Acts 13 and 14 leaves the reader with an impression that Paul did most or nearly all of the missionary action. Yet it is tolerably certain that Barnabas was taking a substantial hand in it, especially where the pagans at Lystra (Acts 14: 10-11) equated Paul with Mercury the messenger but Barnabas with Jupiter, a figure of greater significance with these pagans.

Sailing from Paphos they came to a chain of towns in south-central Asia Minor, firstly to Perga in Pamphylia but here no coastal point is named; Luke notes that John Mark came away at this time, returning to Jerusalem presumably from Paphos. Some have concluded that Mark had merely grown weary of the outreach project, but the limited record of this journeying does not show any reason for that supposition. In the absence of more certain facts it is easier to believe that he was out of humour with Paul. Nothing is noted of any preaching at Perga, but in the next town Antioch in Pisidia. Barnabas and Paul, having entered a synagogue, was invited to speak there. Acts 13:16 says "Then Paul stood up..." but it is unlikely that this was anything other than a joint sermon in which they witnessed to Jesus as the Savior firstly witnessed by John the Baptist in the course of administering a baptism of repentance, slain deliberately and raised from the dead by God, then seen for "many days". The Apostle put certain Old Testament scriptural references behind this witnessing, notably of David, and the general tone of the sermon clearly shows that they were concerned with witnessing only to the Jews. It suggests that the idea of outreach to the Gentiles had not occurred to them thus far, although certainly there were already Gentile Christians at Antioch of which they must have known. It is significant that in all the earliest cases of contact with men of the Gentile nations, as with Cornelius to Simon Peter back in Caesarea and Joppa and Sergius Paulus at Paphos, and now also here at Pisidan Antioch it was a matter of Gentiles approaching the Apostles, not the reverse. Acts 13:42-43 says that religious proselytes made further contact with the Apostles: "The Gentiles besought that they might receive preaching on the next Sabbath". Perhaps in the sermon just given the section Acts. 13: 24-37 reflects Barnabas and verses 38:41 ibid. belong to Paul, because the former part has close familiarity with the units of tradition which arose in formulation during the first few years from the time of the Pentecost, while the latter part gives the earliest known closely personal formulation of Paul's achievement of the doctrine of Justification by Faith which he was to elaborate later, especially to the Romans in the mid-fifties.

Reading the narrative carefully, it emerges that in overall effect the Gentiles liked the combination of Barnabas' topic of repentance unto a receivable salvation and Paul's justification by faith, but many of the Jews (though not all) did not. The effect of the first sermon here was to bring a really large mob to hear them, and "when the Jews saw the multitudes they were filled with envy", resulting in a rising opposition. The inevitable further result was a decision by the Apostles, here especially Paul, to change course ethnically: "It was necessary that the word of God should first have been spoken to you; but seeing ye put it from you, and judge yourselves unworthy of everlasting life, lo, we turn to the Gentiles". This is the central and most important outcome of their tour. Where Luke says at Acts 13:51 that they shook off the dust of their feet against them, it is a quotation of a remembered injunction of Jesus given during His ministry, as at Mark 6:11. However, it was not wholly a voluntary departure in disgust from this town – they were driven out, and this is the first recorded occasion of such hostility, in an exciting period of firsts. Probably much of the hostility in this Region arose from Jewish irritation in the prospect of the blessings of the true Messiah's kingdom being now proposed beyond "the privileged chosen people of God". Aghast at the impudence of these itinerant preachers, local Jewish prejudice against the gospel began, and then escalated. Barnabas and Paul saw the typical human inveteracy of their malice, and their decision for the sincerity and gladness of the Gentiles (acts 13:48) is easy to understand. They were also aware of scriptural authority available behind this decision, by Isaiah 42: 1-6, 49:6 and 60:3, of a Light unto the Gentiles, which had been written seven centuries earlier. At the next town Iconium they had similar experience where, Luke says, they were able to spend some time while the townsfolk were divided in confusion regarding them, the opposition here consisting of both Jews and pagan and Gentiles, and opposition from whose intention to stone them they narrowly escaped by moving on to Lystra and Derbe. At Lystra there was opportunity for a healing miracle which, in being achieved, resulted in pagan assumption that they were gods. Significantly the Apostles used the occasion in the best possible way, to inculcate the lesson that the Living God had not left Himself without witness: the providence of the Creator is evident in His bounty which gives us gladness. They did not ridicule the pagan beliefs as rubbish in the way bigots, and perhaps many of us, would have done, in the excitement of reaction against the error naturally to be expected in the pagans whose ignorance had been no fault of their own. At least to a reasonable extent the Apostles were Christians but the Jews, by contrast, who professed to worship the one True God and who were given the privilege of prophetic revelation – and the duty of carrying it outward to the world of nations – were left without excuse. Probably the pagans at Lystra were crestfallen at the Apostles' refusal to accept the honors intended for them; but the record notes that it was a party of Jews coming from Pisidian Antioch and Iconium who persuaded the Lystrans to join in actual physical opposition in which Paul was stoned into unconsciousness. He seems to have been pulled to safety by Barnabas. Then moving on to the next town Derbe they appear to have preached there without meeting trouble; at this place the population was mixed Greek and Roman under the Cilician king Antiochus IV of Commagene who honored the emperor Claudius.

Certainly the Apostles were courageous, because they then retraced their steps through the towns of Lystra, Iconium and Pisidian Antioch. The Acts narrative says that in these towns they met with sufficient success to be confirming disciples and ordaining community elders; but it is likely that this portion is confused with later success achieved when Paul again traveled through the same chain of towns as recorded in Acts 16: 1-5. Their journey home to Antioch in Syria effectively began at Derbe, the southernmost of the recently visited towns, along a route in a westerly direction through Perga and then Attalia on the coast where they took ship. Derbe is situated only about thirty kilometers west of Paul's old home of Tarsus, but there is never mention of a visit through there.

Arriving at Antioch they made their report, the principal article of which was the confirmation that the Christian outreach now definitely embraced people of the Gentile nations: the days when Christian equals confinement to the Jewish cultural ethos were over. In the course of time amounting to perhaps the year 53 there came to Antioch some concern among those of the Jewish church at Jerusalem, to the extent that an embassy was sent to get Paul and Barnabas and bring them to Jerusalem to answer. In the environment of illiteracy and slow communications and travel in those days the Christian faith facility had come far in the 20 years since the Resurrection, spreading a knowledge as quickly and as far distant as Alexander had carried a field the Greek culture, or as the Roman Caesars their conquests. It had now reached a point of cultural confusion with the Jewish Christians among whom some, whom Acts 15:5 identifies as still belonging to the Pharisee sect as well, insisted on bringing the matter of a necessity to be circumcised as Jews in order to (as still belonging to). The pharisee sect as well, insisted on bringing the matter of a necessity to be (circumcised...) be accepted as Christians. Firstly Simon Peter made answer, that the Holy spirit puts no difference between Jew and Gentile, purifying the hearts of both by faith, and asserted that salvation through the grace of the Lord Jesus Christ is universal where it is accepted in freewill. This was then reinforced by Barnabas and Paul who testified by the work they had already done in this regard. It is probable that the judaizers, having lost their argument when they visited Antioch, hoped that the Jerusalem community as being still a central doctrinal authority would bring down Barnabas and Paul to accord with their cherished position. At this time only three of the original Apostles Simon Peter, John and James the Just appear to have been still at Jerusalem, by Galatians 2:9 whom to Paul "seemed to be pillars" of the Church. But in this letter written about five years after the event Paul gives them credit that "they gave me and Barnabas the right hand of fellowship that we should go unto the heathen, and they unto the circumcision". An agreement favorable to Barnabas and Paul was only right in principle and practice, because it gave freedom from not only the rite of circumcision – which was practiced by innumerable other societies including savages before being applied belatedly to Abraham (Genesis 17:10) – but also from the whole ceremonial law of the Jews in which they themselves had not been in constant obedience. That nation, which should have taken up the duty and privilege of instructing other and benighted nations to whom Christianity was now beginning to be addressed, only sought to isolate itself. Yet is should also be noted that Judaism preserved the prophecies, and its assault on polytheism and idolatry and its proselytizing activities paved the way for Christians success however unintentionally. In particular the cult of the Jewish ceremonial religious machinery could not purge the conscience of the guilt of sin, a fact which Saul Paul had vividly realized at his own Christian beginning.

As head of the Jerusalem Church James therefore summed up in the Apostles' favor, and the first known encyclical letter concerning this matter was taken back to Antioch by the return of Barnabas and Paul with others named as Judas and Silas. By the chronology of the Book of Acts the phenomenon of local Gentiles being more "fired up" by the Christian teaching than were many of the Jews, was experienced before the issue of circumcision arose and was resolved; and this makes the Jewish supposed requirement redundant, apart from other considerations. In Acts 15: 36-39 shortly after the first return to Antioch Paul suggested a second tour along the route they had taken earlier. Here Luke clearly gives what Paul had supplied, as really his only source for it; because it is not easy to see a refusal by Paul to take Mark with them again as sufficient reason for a sharp contention to the extent of their splitting up. More probably Mark had refused to accompany Paul: and with his uncle agreeing with this stand Paul had felt irritated in what would seem to him a double rejection. On the personal side Paul may to some degree have suffered from little-man complex, but it is not charitable to hold that hypothesis. Nevertheless at this time their parting was severe, although by Colossians 4:10 Mark was with Paul again at a much later date. Now essentially alone, Paul found co-workers out on the road where his fortunes were mixed during the next fourteen years. Like salt which is essential to life but too much of it will kill, Paul's zeal in his outreach was at the same time an agency for nourishment but also a potential poison.

Probably it would not be quite wise to regard Saul St. Paul as being comparatively a spiritual giant towering above all other first century luminaries. Such view of him – after the European Reformation- would be as bad as the claim to authoritative direction upon Simon Peter in such position taken without evidence or even probability. Essentially these were ordinary men; but several factors facilitated presentation of Paul to later ages: 1. He was an educated man with an easy familiarity in the activity of writing; 2. As a Hellenistic Jew of the Diaspora he was partly at greater liberty than would be conferred in Judea, and was at ease among Greeks; 3. He had by birth, presumably through his father's line from some past service, the status of Roman citizenship; and 4. Using the Greek lingua franca in unity with his ability to be mobile, he was able to travel quite widely in relation to the practice of those days. But the overwhelmingly significant point about this man, for all his human vagaries lurking below these advantages is, that his conscience-stricken inner thinking after seeing the serene peace of Stephen in Martyrdom, and struggling with a deepening gloom of his self-doubt on religious failure thus far, brought him suddenly to realization and reality in a thunderstorm near Damascus. Luke's Book of Acts (as here in Chapters 9, 22 and 26) was almost certainly picked about in the second century before it came into use in about 180, and the supernatural parts of the Saul conversion narrative ought to be discounted. The verses at Acts 9: 5-6a, of conversation with the sky, is not in the Greek manuscripts, and caution is advised for the Reader at Acts 12: 7-8, 16:26-30, 19: 6-7 and 19: 11-17. Also in the narrative of Acts 21:39, 22: 21 the allowing of a prisoner address had no possibility in the system of the Roman Raj – the flow is "The captain came up and arrested him, giving order that he should be bound with two chains, then asked who he was and what he had done" (21:33) – "finally giving order to take Paul into the soldiers' quarters for examination under the lash" (22:24). Given his state of mind on the Damascus road when he had seen the mystery of intense wrongness in cutting a blameless life short, Saul probably interpreted a peal of thunder as in Hebrew words: Bihimil gahl rasgiki abianluhbaz ainilaozchad "Son of circumcision, the redeeming innocent blood is violated because of thee". In not understanding electric storms, the Ancients attributed them as absolutely Act of God.

This realization conferred upon Saul a gift of humiliation combined with strength, in a remarkable combination of circumstances. Very likely nothing much had happened to him in forty years of settled life at Tarsus where he had lived convinced in his birth-given Hebraic faith whatever its errors, working as a tentmaker by trade but probably also engaging in debates with Stoics. Here we have an intellectual man, impressed already by Greeks who from Socrates, Plato and Aristotle in their long past were learning to think, and as a member of the usual local Jewish minority defensive in its self-conscious national idea, Saul may have participated in the making of proselytes from pagans to

"God-fearers" at Tarsus where a good ideal of it was known to have been done. By Saul's time many Greeks had become dissatisfied with the religious folk lore of their culture and were in search of a possible inner peace potentially to be found in the God of the Jewish doctrine (where Saul failed to find it). There was a drawing together in that locality outside of contemporary wars, where a geography of mixing people up had furnished a society of broadminded character, resembling similar at Antioch. All this environment stands behind the great St. Paul who, in effect, stood upon its gigantic shoulders when he said such thing as "In Christ there is neither Jew nor Greek, for all are one in Him. But all have sinned, and come short of the glory of God; I am made all things to all men, which I may perhaps save some. And by the grace of God, I am what I am". His undoubted linkage with the Greek cultural ethos of Tarsus is visible in his letters, as in Galatians 1:10, 3: 2-8, 3:15-21 and 5: 11-12 where Paul virtually sets up the dynamics of a Plato putting his hearers through a Socratic examination, or at 1 Thessalonians 5: 21-22 where an injunction of secular origin requires a scrutinizing of everything in order to reject what is not good. The God of Abraham was also the God of Plato: "As the First Cause, God is perfectly independent of influences and is immutable. Not ignorant of the affairs of men, He is concerned with them; and through the ordering of Nature, which He sustains, He sees that Justice is always done". Paul himself is reflected in this Greek mirror at Acts 17: 22-31 in his speech at Athens. The short Chapter 13 as presented of First Corinthians is practically a Stoic poem; but the clarity of his conviction which came out of his experience in deep self-examination towards Damascus, stands beyond either the ancient Jewish bunk or the contemporary Stoic wisdom: "More than ever I delight to boast of the weaknesses that humiliate me, so that the strength of Christ may enshrine itself in me. I am well content with these humiliations with the insults, the hardships and persecutions in times of difficulty I undergo for Christ. When I am weakest in one sense, then I am strongest of all" (Second Corinthians 12: 9-10).

No doubt St. Paul was exceptional to a degree because of the circumstances from which he came, and he did seize opportunities as they were given to him in the course of his Christian career, playing well the cards dealt to him, so to speak. But after being early rejected in the Jerusalem Church in 40 when the brethren sent him back home to Tarsus, it was likely for him to have simply remained there. We owe a great deal to Stephen in the first place, from whose martyrdom Saul paused to reflect very seriously on what they were doing, and to Barnabas in the second place for his dogged diplomacy in the confidence of bringing Saul back into circulation (to Antioch) and pushing forward the idea of travel. Similarly much is owed to the Greek cultural ethos in regard to all of them. Further, if Paul did dream ambitiously of a Christian Roman Empire by the time he came to write to the Romans in 56 – which is possible – he was clearly, from his type of the wild olive grafted on the civilized Jewish rootstock (Romans 11:16-24), unaware of the difference between the Greeks with whom he certainly succeeded and the Romans with whom he did not. In the light of Christ's warning that the world is to remain as it is, down to the end time appointed, recorded in the thirteenth of Mark where we are enjoined to remain always on watch, we learn from the model which Paul's experience and example presents that nonetheless all possibility for increase of heaven's kingdom is open to the heart of the individual. It is useful to grace across Paul in this way before we now reach into a general survey of that great inheritance, the corpus of his surviving letters. If he could "time warp" into this twenty-first century, what might he say to us now? "The human heart is minutely treacherous and animal instincts burn in it, but it does not make itself; if there is a soul leprosy in the loved and laughing infant, who knows what it might turn into? This is a world of the sinning state having no good thing of itself to redeem it, unchanged since the night of ignorance was far spent, the day of salvation already at hand, in Nero's Rome. After centuries professed churches accommodate every rotten thing (vide Romans 1: 26-27) against which we in the first century were specific. Despise ye the Church of God and shame us? In this I praise you not. In lip-service the centuries have counted time as years of our Lord, ostensibly claiming to ride in the name of Christ Jesus of Nazareth. You may claim it; but in whose name do you ride?"

4
The Facility of St. Paul's known Letters

Luke knew Paul, but not his letters even though the Epistles were clearly intended for public reading, which suggests that the author of the Book of Acts was not present in the churches to which they were addressed.

The flavor of Paul's personality pervades the letters; salvation in and through Christ is the central and constant theme in all of them while making connection to all topics as taken up secondarily. Other brethren are included by name in joint greetings, but the letters are not of any joint authorship; and the giving of exhortations of a general nature near the close of a letter was a common practice of the time, with examples similarly appearing at the signing-off in Peter, James and Hebrews. To Corinth Paul was writing replies to matters which the correspondence brought to him, and we owe a great deal to the community members there who thus in effect were drawing him out. In these return communications he interposed preaching with views of his own position, and used Old Testament texts generally but most frequently in the Epistle to the Romans. Altogether such texts are quoted at Galatians 3: 6-13, 4:22, 4:30; First Corinthians 1:19, 2:9, 3:19-20, 9:9, 10: 1-5, 10: 8-12, 14:21, 15:55; Second Corinthians 6:16-18, 8:15, 9:9, 13:1b; Romans 1:17b, 3:12-18, 4:1-3, 4:7, 4: 9b-13, 4: 18-22, 9: 8-18, 9:25-29, 9:33, 10:5, 10:15-21, 11:2-5, 11:8-10, 11:26-27, 12:19b, 14:11, 15:3 and 15:9-12.

Very likely Paul would have done better, especially in Rome, if he had minimised his Jewish References, but that is easy to see in hindsight. It is possible that a familiarity with Gospel units collected by Luke may be one of the factors of difference in his late letters written at Rome (col. 1:9-10, 1:23, 1:28, 2:3 and 3:13, Phil. 1:9-11 and 4:8-9) from the corpus of the earlier letter; for these parts refer to general gospel knowledge "of which I Paul am made a Minister."

Paul does not guard himself against being taken out of context, and in using his letters it is important to hold the context of a particular remark, remembering that the writer has his correspondents in mind and may omit units of their mutual familiarity. He was reflecting the mood of the moment, not writing for the future. As an impetuous and emotional man, Paul did not watch his words carefully as he consciously discharged a full central inspiration within his wide capacity of feeling utter humility at some times, but expressing strong assertion of self assurance at others. To make estimates of the dates when the Epistles were written is no easy matter. That Galatians was the earliest is possible from 1. The autobiographical fragment in Gal. 1:13 to 2:16 being far less likely in any letter after the first which in effect introduce him as an epistolary author; 2. Reflecting back from his young days there is a Greek-looking approach in Galatians as if to set up a debating position in which he asks the recipients to demonstrate their model if they were meaning towards "another gospel"; and 3. The irate tone in parts of Galatians would be more characteristic of novelty in the correspondence method, if up till now Paul had been accustomed to using an oral delivery with brethren who were present. If Galatians 2: 1-10 refers to the same Jerusalem visit and involvement as Acts 15: 1-29, Paul's statement of fourteen years gives the earliest date for Galatians at mid-54, setting up a prospect that Thessalonians, at least four Corinthian letters and Romans were written in the period 54 to 57.

Simon Peter at Lydda
Acts. 9:38

Thus it is fair to take the date of the conference on circumcision as the year 54. Evidently Barnabas had at some time returned to Antioch; and Titus, noted in Galatians as "a Greek" but more probably a Roman, is never mentioned in the Book of Acts. In glancing through the confusion about circumcision it may be best to take up Luke's account in Acts 15 although it is out of chronological sequence, and then review what Paul says in the connection at the Second of Galatians. At some time in the period of the last ten years news of successes being gradually manifest in the Christian outreach to Gentiles in Galatia, Macedonia and Corinth had reached the Jewish church at Jerusalem where some of the brethren formed the idea that conversion of such people must require their baptism in the Jewish way. Attributing the achievement of the outreach rightly to Paul and Barnabas they accordingly sent a deputation to Antioch to forcibly represent this idea, and of course in view of the experience of these missionary Apostles it resulted in immediate controversy: the judaizing objection could not be accepted. The parties in this dispute then decided to go to Jerusalem, where Acts 15:4 notes that the Church made them welcome, especially in a general appreciation of the work they were doing. Upon an inevitable motion from brethren identified as Pharisees, to bring a requirement for circumcision universally "to keep the law of Moses", a conference was convened. This was an important moment in the Christian interest when, in the ancient environment of illiteracy, ignorance and slow travel this faith following had traveled comparatively far without loss thus far, but was now crashing into confusion at its original centre.

In the procedure of the conference Simon Peter firstly answered, that the Holy Spirit puts no difference between Jews and Gentiles: that all hearts are purified by faith, in that salvation is universally given where it is accepted in freewill. This apostle was certainly qualified to witness thus, from his having given ministry along exactly these lines as described in Acts 9:32 – 10:48, after which he had himself faced judaizing opposition upon having received Gentiles uncircumcised (Acts 11: 2-3), but verse 18 ibid indicates that his defense over it had put the matter to rest. After hearing Simon Peter the conference kept silence and listened to Barnabas and Paul as they gave answer, similarly testifying to the right validity of their position by describing the evangelical work they had already done. In their working experience the Gentiles had usually been more actively receptive to the Christian teaching, especially the Greeks, than were many of the Jews in those days before questions of circumcision were pushed forward. The matter did not arise with them and indeed, there is room for doubt as to whether the rite of circumcision ever had any efficacy at all. It was practiced before the time of the Hebrew Tribes among Egyptians and even among savages, and may have been adopted by the Hebrews as a means of distinguishing themselves from neighboring Philistines who did not practice it, but the rite came into importance among the Jews only after their Babylonian Exile when the Torah Books were either written or updated Paul believed in the Torah accounts regardless of what might not be factual therein (as for instance the body of legal code antedating

Moses by centuries), and held from their faith the plain formula that in any case law was superseded in fulfillment by Divine grace, and consequently even if the text is garbled between Genesis 17: 1-4 and 17: 9-14 circumcision in any religion sense is of the heart and cannot be represented in anything physical. It is easy to imagine him saying at this conference, "Please, please can we stop arguing about this? It doesn't matter".

Perhaps the judaizers at Jerusalem, spiritually blind and deaf in the context of the uncircumcised heart (vide Deuteronomy 10:16 and 30:6, Jeremiah 9: 25-26) hoped, having lost their cause at Antioch, that the Jerusalem doctrinal authorities would bring down Barnabas and Paul into line with their cherished position. At Galatians 2:7 Paul says that only three of the primary Apostles, as "pillars of the Church" were present: Simon Peter, John Zebedee and James the Just. In Acts 15: 13-21 James, as head of the Jerusalem Church summed up on the basis of a precedent having already been set, in the work done with success toward accommodating uncircumcised Gentiles by Simon Peter which in turn rested upon a certainty that God viewed the Gentile nations favorably, in their understanding, from knowledge of the Classical Prophets. Here James may have been slightly misquoting, if Luke is accurate verbatim, but in any event the judaizers could not have it both ways: the coming of the Messiah was promised and the Gentiles were accepted, in the Messianic Texts of the prophets; there was no case for any selecting of parts a la carte which might appeal in later opinion while rejecting anything humanly disliked. By the Jerusalem Apostles it was expected that the Gentiles would, under grace yet keep cleanliness in observing similar legalistic living standards. Upon James' summary an encyclical letter was drafted, which Luke quotes as Acts 156: 23-29, effectively releasing the Christian faith system from Jewish limits and involving an admission that the judaizers who started the excitement at Antioch had not been officially commissioned to their action (15:24). The letter was then taken to Antioch by men named as Judas and Silas traveling with the returning Paul and Barnabas.

Of this occasion Paul says at Galatians 2:7-10 "Those who reputed to be the main support of the Church, James and Cephas and John, saw plainly that I was commissioned to preach unto the uncircumcised, as Cephas" (Simon Peter)" was to the circumcised. He whose power had enabled Cephas to become the Apostle of the circumcised had enabled me to be an Apostle to the Gentiles. Thus, recognizing the grace given me by God, they joined their right hands in fellowship with Barnabas and myself. The Gentiles were to be our province, the circumcised theirs; only we were to remember the poor, which indeed I had set myself to do".

This whole matter of universal liberation in Christianity is fundamental. By His revelation of the mercy and love of God to human brotherhood Christ has made it possible for us to consciously put our trust in God. In the Christian system there is a future to all who have the virtue to repent and the energy to atone; and wherever a seed of affection is sown, some weed of selfishness is uprooted to make way for it.

As being a diatribe of post-circumcision value against judaizing, the Epistle to the Galatians strongly moves toward a probability that the recipients of the letter were mostly and perhaps all originally Jews. There is little here of any address to Greek or Roman ex-pagans, although Gal. 5: 19-23 indicates the presence of an antinomian party of some kind. At Galatians 2: 21 and 5:2 the central topic of the letter is well summarized: "If we could be justified by the ancient law, then Christ's death would be in vain... I guarantee that in your being circumcised" (i.e. under the law) "Christ is of no value to you". This gives an impression that Paul had received a report that men in the Galatians region were being added to the community he had successfully established on his second tour there, but now in an involvement of the Jewish circumcision rite instead of by baptism in the universal faith of Christ.

It is highly likely that this kind of news reached him shortly after the conference on circumcision at Jerusalem described in

Acts 15: 1-29, when it would have struck Paul with some force; he had succeeded at Jerusalem, and now this apparently first successfully made community was slumping straight back into the past. This would go some way towards explaining why he did not simply shrug off the matter as a bad job, leaving them abandoned in the course they were choosing, plus the fact that by this time he had found substantial success with Gentile communities elsewhere. To write a letter was natural in the fact that judaizers from Jerusalem were active in traveling with a purpose of upholding the old position (Acts 15:1) It is possible that such men had gone quickly to Galatia when their efforts in the Jerusalem conference were thwarted (ref. Galatians 1:9 and 4:17), a thesis in which Paul would certainly realize a necessity to affirm his apostolic authority as deriving independently from the Jerusalem Apostles, and hence he gave the biographical resume. Also, the peculiar verse at Gal. 5:11 gives a strong hint that someone was lying in pretending that Paul had been supportive of the circumcision rite elsewhere, and long since: "If I, brethren, still preach circumcision, why am I still persecuted?" Judaizers belonging to the region could not bring this; and the unity of believers was also a deep concern of Paul, in which he would certainly see the judaizers of recent memory as a divisive element against the Apostles' cordial support in the outcome of the conference. Jerusalem judaizers viewed Paul as an enemy, denying that he had any authority to preach freedom from the law, and no doubt (if indeed they did go to Galatia) they would be engaged in argument against such of the Galatians brethren who could point to Paul's close association with the Jerusalem Apostles, to some extent defending his record among them; and some peculiar ambiguities in the Epistle should be read in the prospect of this possibility (as at, for example, 4:12, 4: 19-20, 5:7-8, 6:12-13), because he was earnestly appealing against both unfair attack and false defense by those who misunderstood him. His understandable eager haste to take up the matter by writing perhaps explains why there is no thanksgiving after the opening salutation; together with his remark near the close (at 6:11) "You see what a large letter I have written for you in my own hand", this seems to point also to the earliest of the Epistles: there were longer letters to come.

Galatians consist broadly in three sections: The biography component, Chapters 1 and 2; Appeals made by referencing back to the Scriptures, in Chapters 3 and 4 which would form a prototype for similar in Romans; and Units of ethical discourse, in Chapters 5 and 6 bearing a Sermon-on-the-Mount aspect, to reappear in Thessalonians and Corinthians. The high points in this Epistle are at:

2:17 – Though we are sinners seeking to be justified by Christ, Christ is not the minister of sin"; 3: 28 – "There is nether Jew nor Greek, nor any other distinction: for ye are all one in Jesus Christ"; 5:13 – "Ye have been called into liberty not to use this liberty for fleshly purposes, but to serve one another, by loving" with 5:24 – "And they that are Christ's have crucified the lusts and affections of the flesh"; 6:7- Be not deceived: God is not mocked. Whatsoever a man soweth, that shall he reap" with 6:9 – "And let us not be weary in well doing; for in due season we shall reap, if we faint not"; and 6:14 – "God forbid that I should glory, save in the cross of our Lord Jesus Christ, by whom the world is crucified unto me, and I unto the world".

The letter presented in the canon as Second Thessalonians is not considered here as by St. Paul. In it the stress upon negative outcomes awaiting the ungodly is not his; indeed it amounts to a wholesale reversal of Paul's positive emphasis on the prospect of glorious joy to be manifest in the Lord's coming to the faithful. This letter shows literary dependence on the earlier genuine letter. Also whereas in 1 Thessalonians 1:10, 3:13 and possibly 4:13f and 5:23 Paul clearly still held a view that the Second Coming of Christ was perhaps a near possibility, 2 Thessalonians 1:7-10 envisages the Second Coming as in a far future, here teaching by a word-picture drawn up in notably un-Pauline language. Only a short period of time elapsed between the two letters, and in this clumsy addition of Paul's name there is no sign that they could be sent by the same writer to the same community in these circumstances. Again, it was not Paul's habit to repeat himself as for instance with 1 Thess. 1:6, 2 Thess. 1:4 on persecutions, or to quickly say something opposite as for instance 1 Thess. 1:8, 2 Thess. 1:11 "your faith in God has overflowed everywhere, so that we do not need to speak a word" against "We are always praying for you, that God may find you worthy of your vocation". It may be, that the second letter was a forgery attempting to use Paul's standing as a means of pushing forward the writer's own doctrine.

That First Thessalonians was written soon after Galatians is a possibility in the contrasting relief visible with Paul's thankfulness in regard to this loyal little community (1 Thess. 1:2-8, 2:1, 2:13-16, 3:6-12). By 2:14-16 the writer models a reminder on something recent, in reference to judaizers who "try to hinder us from preaching salvation to the Gentiles' – in the present tense; and the spontaneous and spirited style continues the spirited mode in Galatians only now it is manifest positively, instead of being delivered in censure. Neither doctrinally theological, sermonic, nor answering community enquiries, this was a personal letter joyfully written in the twin feelings of relief and pleasure. Since Paul had resorted to using the pen which, unlike Barnabas he found easy, he could write a letter in a compensating satisfaction after having done one in deep concern. There is even a Stoic echo at 1 Thess. 5:21-22 in the injunction – of secular origin – to scrutinize everything in order to reject what is not good.

The Epistles were written spontaneously, and not edited. As a reason behind the letter to the Galatians, Paul surely would feel an indignation upon hearing that a community for which he had made substantial efforts in the scope of three extended visits, had lapsed into accommodating men immersed in errors; it meant that his efforts in that region had been all for nothing. The reason for doing a letter to Thessalonica was his gratitude for that community's evidently contrasting loyalty giving grounds for hope: in Paul's experience beyond Antioch this had been the earliest such. Now a third reason for writing arises with the

Corinthians where the letters were one-half of a two-way correspondence in which the brethren sought guidance in specifics arising in a rapidly growing church very largely Greek. The Epistles to Corinth did not originally consist as they were later presented; indeed there is no certainty that Paul's letters all survived to be collected as a total entirety. There were at least four Corinthian letters, and it is first necessary to pull out the fragments which have been mixed together, in order to read the surviving parts and thereby gain some understanding of the business in hand. The following collation appears to reconstruct four letters of Paul to Corinth:

First Corinthians written at Ephesus in 54: 1 Cor. 10: 1-10: 23. This Epistle is referred at 1 Cor. 5:9, that is, in

Second Corinthians written at Ephesus in late 54: 1 Cor. 1:1-9: 27 plus 10:24-16:24. A reply to the first letter is acknowledged at 1 Cor. 7:1 and a visit to Corinth is proposed at 1 Cor. 16: 1-8. After this visit,

Third Corinthians written at Ephesus in 55: 2 Cor. 10: 1-13:10. Another visit is proposed at 2 Cor. 12:14; Acts 20:2-3 gives 3 months duration in it.

Fourth Corinthians written either at Ephesus or on Paul's journey to Jerusalem in late 56 or early 57: 2 Cor. 1: 1-9:15 plus 13: 11-14. Third Corinthians is referred at 2 Cor. 2:3-4 and 7:12.

The Epistles to the Corinthians show quite a lot of the teaching given in churches before the gospel accounts were written, even though Paul was not writing for future Christian historians; it is a fortunate incidental light. The first letter clearly had been occasioned by some report attended with questions, but the usual opening section had been lost in the far past. The second letter appears to be complete as constituted here, in which Paul dealt with many more questions – this function seems to have been encouraged from the reception of the first letter not long before –the missionary taking also the occasion to give substantial preaching; they were encouraging each other. In the third letter the opening greeting is again lost; from the censorious content of this letter it any be reasonably inferred that Paul had received some report of irreligious dealings, activities, or behavior in this important community. He followed up the letter with a visit of reasonable length. The fourth letter has the appearance of being spontaneous, not occasioned as a reply to anything received but rather consisting in Paul's desire to summarise his position with the Corinthians as he was preparing to go to Jerusalem and then possibly Rome for a visit there long intended. If the signing-off at 2 Cor. 13:11-14 does belong here this letter again seems to be complete, from a space of perhaps two years between it and the third letter; an intention of altering his plan from Corinth to Jerusalem appears at 2 Cor. 1:15-16, and the fourth letter is in fact a long farewell to the Corinthians. The high points in Corinthians are at:

(1st) 1 Cor. 10:13 – "There hath no temptation taken you but such as is common to man; but God is faithful, who will not suffer you to be tempted above that ye are able, but will make a way to escape, that ye may be able to resist it".

(2nd) 1 Cor. 1:9 – "God is faithful, by Whom ye were called into the fellowship of His Son, Jesus Christ our Lord"; 1:24 – "And unto them which are called, whether Jews or Gentiles, Christ is the power and wisdom of God"; 2:4-5 – "And my speech and my preaching is not with enticing words of man's wisdom, but in demonstrating of the Spirit and of power: that your faith should not stand in the wisdom of men, but in the power of God"; 3:6 – One man plants, another gives the watering; but God gives the increase"; 4:20 – "And the kingdom of God is not in word, but in power"; 15:56-57 – "The sting of death is sin, and the strength of sin is the law; but thanks be to God, who giveth us the victory through our Lord Jesus Christ.

(4th) 2 Cor. 4:18 – "We look not at the things which are seen, but to the things which are not seen; for the things which are seen are only temporal, but the things which are not seen are eternal"; 5:7 – "For we walk by faith, not by sight"; 5:17 – If any man be in Christ, he is a new creature. Old things are passed away: behold, all things are become new"; 9:15 – "Thanks be to God for His inexpressible gift".

St. Paul's Epistles are largely sermonic, but there is a great deal of human emphasis coming from opinions earlier formed, and at times the level of writing does rise to a plane of representing the grace of God in Christ. It is in the letters to the Corinthian community that we find facility of benefit thus to be cherished, most readily to hand. In general these, and particularly the second as presented here having most of First Corinthians of the canon, are useful in showing the early and growing local Christian community and the attendant problems met by efforts to "square the circle" in fusing worship with socializing by building institutional facilities to which the holy gospel does not point.

The Epistle to the Romans was written at Corinth probably during Paul's three-month visit there which, if true, would date it in 55. The mention of one Phoebe of the Corinthian community at Romans 16:1, apparently the bearer of another letter to Ephesus, supports this hypothesis. Romans is the only one of St. Paul's Epistles in the nature of a treatise, being written as a project to clarify his position to the small community of Jewish Christians at Rome in an intention to visit the city himself when this should become possible. There are also signs that he was thinking of spending the rest of his life there; at Romans 15:24 and 28 the translators' assumption of "Spain" is absurd – it is of fifteenth century European origin, the Ancients called that country Iberia; the Greek term spanian is something else.

The large part devoted to the doctrine of Justification by Faith in this Epistle shows Paul's past experience of enjoying divine acceptance by which his former past was done away, as with the wayward son accounted as righteous when he acted upon belief in the love of his father in Christ's parable of the prodigal Son. It

The Facility of St. Paul's known Letters 59

is a beginning. Additionally Paul wanted to deal here on a broad canvas, which is exemplified in the block of text at Romans 1:18-32 with horrible word-pictures of present day familiarity, showing his own acquaintance with the notorious immorality of the time. By Christ's death considered as a sacrifice, sin is cancelled; and in the third of Romans we find the earliest assertion of this, as far as is known, upon Isaiah 53:4f the Righteous Servant by Whose stripes we are healed. The middle Chapters here 5 to 8 inclusive furnish the clearest picture of what Christianity meant to St. Paul; but in Romans 15:12-21 and 9:4-13 with 11:1-4 he clearly remained immersed in the ancient Jewish folk tale epics with which the Christian need have no concern. The same thing is true of the author of the Book of Hebrews: in the prospect that Apollos was its author it is interesting to use Hebrews against Romans as comparing Apollo's with Paul, as vide 1 Corinthians 1:10-16, 4:6 and 4: 15-16 on rival factions at Corinth. With this letter to the Roman Christians the fact that Paul was and continued to be fundamentally a Jew, to whom the blindness of his countrymen seemed unnatural and it was painful to him, is most forcibly brought home to us: this for which we normally have little thought. At Romans 15:19-24 Paul appears to indicate a feeling that his missionary travels were about finished. The doxology in 16:25-27 is a later addition, and the rest of Chapter 16 is part of a letter not to Rome but to Ephesus, sent to Paul's many acquaintances there from Corinth where Caius was a city official. The high points in Romans are at:

1:16 – "I am not ashamed of the gospel of Christ; for it is the power of God unto salvation, to every one that believeth"; 3: 21-24 – "but now the righteousness of God is manifested beyond the law, witnessed by the law and the prophets: by faith of Jesus Christ unto and upon all them that believe, for there is no difference in that all have sinned and come short of the glory of God. But justified freely by His grace through the redemption that is in Christ Jesus" with 3:28 "therefore we conclude that a man is justified by faith without the deeds of the law"; 5:5- "And hope maketh not ashamed; because the love of God is shed abroad in our hearts by the Holy Ghost which is given unto us"; 8:31-32 + 8:35 – "If God be for us, who can be against us? He that spared not His own Son, but delivered Him up for us all, how should He not, together with Him, also give us freely all things? Nothing shall be able to separate us from the love of God which is in Christ Jesus our Lord"; 11:36 – "For of, through, and to Him are all things, to Whom be glory forever. Amen".

These are the letters of Paul written during his Ephesus period c. mid-54 to early 57. Later, in the early sixties he wrote from Rome to communities at Philippi and Colossae, also personally to Philemon at the latter. Philippians 1:13 and 4:22 suggests Rome as the place of writing, where Paul was living under restraints amounting to imprisonment (Acts 28:16, Phil. 1: 12-14), although the terms 'praetorium' and 'the emperor's household' could apply at other places. By Phil 1:1 and 2:19 Timotheus was still with Paul in the later days, and by Colossians 4:10 and 4:14 Mark and Luke as well. Although Philippians is a closely affectionate letter of concern, these letters make no doctrinal addition to the letters written before Paul went to Rome; however, Phil. 2: 6-11 has the appearance of a late stage in his doctrinal development. Colossae was a church never visited by Paul, but probably Epaphras, who came from there, asked him to write for this community in general terms with intent of strengthening against heresy. In these late letters there is a general atmosphere of Paul coming to believe that he would be dying at the location of the writing.

St. Paul's contribution was large, important, and interesting, though by no means the whole story. The kingdom of heaven is within the believer who accepts God's gift in faith belief, whereupon God accepts him. No doubt Christianity would have continued onward with Barnabas, Simon Peter, Apollos, Mark, Timothy and St. John without Paul and Luke, as it did; but we should have been then poorer, without Paul's letters.

5
St. Paul's Travels in 44-59

It is with St. Paul perhaps more than with any other early Christian writer that we must view his work against the first century environment of mixed Greek and Oriental syncretism in which, as a Hellenistic Jew of the diaspora, Paul belonged. His letters were written spontaneously as he traveled with what he called merimna (care, or concern) "of all the churches" (2 Corinthians 11:28). Why was he inclined to travel? The itinerant example of Christ and His commissioning of the followers to go out into the world, recorded in the gospels, sets the stage against the idea of a central Church station, but this directing was not visible to Paul until later; and by his assertion in Galatians 2:6 that the Apostles at Jerusalem "added nothing to me" in which he was clearly unimpressed, he does not seem to have acquired extensive knowledge of the gospel history materials. He does not show details of such in his letters. Where, in his earliest letter he refers immediately to preaching of the gospel of Christ at Galatians 1:6f it is of course his own aspect of gospel which is involved, not as we would automatically understand as beginning from St. Mark, the earliest history not yet written. As a pioneer in formulating the doctrine and ethics of his gospel, Paul's composite message consisted in teaching the centrality of Christ; it was the central thread through all his letters, which for him was rooted in a Jewish-derived realization of the plan and purpose of God, in which he had personally left the religion of Jewry behind in his progress. St. Paul's key in manifestation emerged at the moment, whenever it was, of his realizing a sense of Gentile mission: in effect the reborn Jew upon whom the confirmation of the universality of Christ had come with some force. It was as a man apostolically independent by means of God's action in Christ that, not consciously forsaking Judaism in the sense of converting from one religion to another he sought, in being "all things to all men" (1 Corinthians 9:22) to justify the believer in Christ Jesus as itself a gospel principle.

Paul himself gives a resume of why he undertook to travel in this regard, in Romans 15:16-20: "That I should be the minister of Jesus Christ to the Gentiles, ministering the gospel of God, that the offering up of the Gentiles might be acceptable, being sanctified by the Holy Ghost. I have therefore whereof I may glory through Jesus Christ in those things which Christ hath not wrought by me, to make the Gentiles obedient, by word and deed, through mighty signs and wonders, by the power of the Spirit of God; so that from Jerusalem, and round about unto Illyricum, I have fully preached the gospel of Christ. Yea, so have I strived to preach the gospel, not where Christ was named (or, known), lest I should build upon another man's foundation". Paul was thinking along ancient Hebrew lines of the functions of their priesthood, this simile now involving Christ's choice of him, as he certainly believed, as an instrument beyond that old order: if he had any ground for glorifying it was not in himself but in the unmerited and rich favor of Jesus. Indeed there is a lesson for all times future to him in this; for it would always be a truly noble ambition for innumerable men in Christendom who must needs generally build on foundations already laid, if only they had taken infinite pains to so build the Christian progress that their superstructures would not disgrace the immense holy rectitude of the Christian system which possessed such pure floral glory and beautiful simplicity along its beginning.

A considerable body of knowledge about Paul's movements was made available by the fortunate circumstance of Luke's association, from which St. Luke was able not only to use Paul's reminiscences as a source but could also add his own first-hand experiences from that association in compiling the second half of his Book of Acts. It is regrettable that the decades across the first century did not supply similar combinations – not least because this dearth leaves an impression that St. Paul was so much head-and-shoulders above all other contemporary luminaries, an idea that is quite wrong – excellent though Paul's witness was; we cannot get the desirable facility of comparison.

At Antioch Paul had suggested a second missionary tour through the towns which he and Barnabas had earlier visited, with a purpose of discovering the extent of survival in the religious interest there, and of any progress in it. Acts 15:40-41ff says that from the point here of splitting up with Barnabas he departed with one of the brethren lately from Jerusalem named Silas, who had come to Antioch after the conference on circumcision. The note of them going "through Syria and Cilicia" indicates a route by land, probably passing between Caesarea and Tarsus, but neither town is mentioned, by which they came to Derbe and then Lystra just to the north-west of it. At Lystra one Timotheus joined with Paul and Silas, a man mentioned by Paul at 1 Corinthians 4:17, 17:14, 18:5, 19:22, 20:4, Romans 16:21, Philippians 1:1 and 2:19, Colossians 1:1, 1 Thessalonians 1:1 and 3:2 and thus one of apparently prominent standing in Paul's retinue. There has long been, and still is, extraordinary confusion of this man's identity with that of St. Timothy, an entirely different individual. The two names are differenced in the Greek as Timotheou and Timotheon respectively, although at one point 2 Corinthians 1:1 this spelling is breached. Fortunately, some indication of their antecedents is given, notably in two unconnected places. Timotheus' mother was a Jewess (Acts 16:1), but at 2 Timothy 1:5 – a letter not written by Paul – Timothy's mother Eunike and grandmother Lois were, by these names, certainly Greek; and where the writer says (2 Timothy 3:15) that he knew of Timothy's upbringing from childhood in the Christian faith, and points (3:11

ibid) to afflictions suffered at Antioch in Pisidia, Iconium and Lystra (Acts 14:19-20) it indicates Barnabas as the only candidate for writing to Timothy. It also suggests Cyprus, from Acts 4:36, as the land of Timothy's original home.

But, I digress. Paul is said to have agreed to circumcision for Timotheus at Lystra to please the local Jews, which in view of his stoutly maintained position against continuance of the rite elsewhere, is rather surprising. In Galatians 2:1-3 Paul himself notes that Titus, one of the brethren at Antioch and a Gentile, had been protected against undergoing the rite of circumcision in Jerusalem indeed in the course of Paul's' opposition at the conference. Additionally the narrative in Acts is specific with a detail that in this group of towns Paul and Silas issued the contents of the Encyclical letter of Acts 15:23-29 by which an established freedom from the formerly held law requirements for acceptance, though not from all food kosher laws, was made known. Perhaps Timotheus had requested the rite. Luke notes that in these places the population of believers increased and churches were established, but does not describe anything of what the churches comprised; but it is reasonable to assume that each of these early and remote churches consisted of a small gathering of believers assembling at points outside of the synagogues of regular Jewish worship, possibly in each other's homes as they still did at Corinth, for instance, in the fifties. With the text at Acts 16:6-7 there is some doubt as to whether, after traveling beyond Pisidian Antioch in a north-westerly direction there actually was a divine unction forbidding them access to the Bithynia district on the Asia Minor north coast. It is overwhelmingly probable that a down-to-earth reason constituted the cause in dissuading them and Luke, not then being present, lacked the necessary detail and was obliged to fudge the matter, though not deliberately.

However, it seems certain that Luke, to whom Paul refers as "the beloved physician" at Colossians 4:14 was present in Paul's retinue thereafter, if the sudden and permanent change from they (the retinue) to we at Acts 16:7-10 is unconsciously literal in the writing as normally expected. Often there were circumstances where early Christians preferred to avoid inserting their own personal names in a written work, as with St. John at John 13:23 or 20: 2-8; and here "the vision" is just as stated: a Macedonian, probably a Gentile, who had crossed the narrow strait of the Bosphorus – easily assumed to be Luke himself. Beyond this point in the narrative the whole flow is much clearer in detail. Paul's reaction to the "vision in the night", as something more than a poetic expression, was to conclude a belief that it was in the Lord's purpose for them to carry the new faith knowledge and belief into Europe; and by this single decision he became the great Apostle to the West. They seem to have lost no time in traveling along the north coast of the Aegean Sea to spend some time at Philippi, one of the principal Macedonian towns, preaching here to women who, as Luke says they resorted to a spot outside the town, may possibly have been outcasts not unlike the Samaritan woman featured in the fourth of John, one of whom became their hostess in this place. Certainly one damsel had need of an exorcising, according to Acts 16: 16-18; and the effect of a successful remedy by Paul in this case was that Paul and Silas, as the "ringleaders", were brought before the local magistrates as Jewish rabble rousers. Reaching successful outcomes with many of the Gentiles was clearly not going to be easy or automatic. In the example furnished here the narrative in Acts 16:26-30 is garbled; the best probability is, that one or more of the prison guards heard either Paul or Silas out and was satisfied by receiving a good explanation of what they were in fact up to, a satisfaction carried through to the magistrates to the extent of some degree of conversion. This probability combines with the concern of the local authority on discovering that they had Roman citizenship (Acts 16:38).

The route of Paul's retinue now passed southward in West Greece, which is identical with modern Greece, the western half of Asia Minor comprising East Greece in apostolic times. At the northern end of this route they soon met trouble at Thessalonica when Paul aspired to preach in the Jewish synagogue which would have been an action better avoided on the basis that with Barnabas elsewhere he had so done. Nothing much is known of the man Jason in this place, himself perhaps a Jew if identical with the Jason named at Romans 16:21 as a kinsman of Paul, but the mob clearly saw him as one connected in the Christian outreach, since they dragged him to the authorities when they failed to find Paul and Silas. Very likely these latter had already left for the next town Berea, because the Jews at Thessalonica now sent "certain lewd fellows of the baser sort" after them. Luke says that Silas and Timotheus remained at Berea, but Paul went onward to Athens and awaited them there. The detail does not give any clue as to why they were temporarily split up, but it is likely that Paul was the man they were after, as seems to have been the case earlier with the assault on Paul and Barnabas in the three Galatians towns of Acts 14:19-20 when only Paul appears to have been dragged about and rendered unconscious.

Paul's general address to learned citizens at Athens forms a fine component of general theological witness, showing his awareness of the cultural importance and value of this place which even in those days was the chief city of the Greek world, certainly intellectually. Perhaps because of this no attempt was made to establish a Christian community there at the time, nor for long afterwards – culturally it would be simply too much to undertake. In the address given in Acts 17: 22-31 the inscription text "To the Unknown God" is more likely to have been worded "To gods of Asia and Europe and Africa, gods unknown and alien", involving the pagan plural, since here a monotheistic singular is highly likely. But in any event it shows a propensity for the local and contemporary men to be honoring unknown and invisible gods for benefits assumed to be received from their hands, and apparently Paul understood this. It is an important point, for similar inscriptions have been found similarly with plurality of the gods, and when Christianity was presented to the Greeks it was new to them in being monotheistic and at the same time no longer Jewish as a religious proposition. It may well be, that elements from Athens immediately responding to Paul's address (vide Acts 17:32-33) paved the way for a Christian beginning at Corinth, at no great distance since it was only a matter of some weeks future to this activity when two Jews Aquila and Priscilla, expelled from Rome under an edict of Claudius in 49, came to Corinth and then Paul was able to meet with some success when he joined them there, according to Acts 18:4.

These missionary travels occupied much more time than is quickly apparent from a regular reading of the Book of Acts. The period between Paul's departure from Antioch with Silas in the spring of 44 and his arrival at Corinth in the Spring of 50 is six years. Luke's project to set down a limited history is not expected to say anything about times and places in which circumstances had not raised or enabled any acts; and almost certainly long periods intervened in which they sought for teaching and conversion opportunities and found none – again an impression that all their time was packed with activities would be quite wrong. Certainly a drawn out and drab prospect was likely in the first leg of the tour through Syria and Cicilia before they reached the Galatian towns previously visited by Paul, in which case he would suffer a feeling of disappointment on failing to break any new ground, and still more on the longer stretch of rough country traversing central Asia Minor from Antioch in Pisidia to Troas on the Bosphorus. Here the route lay across several sub-regions: Pamphylia, Galatia with Pisidia, Asia (that is, including Phrygia and Lydia) beyond which lay Bithynia coastally on the north. It was in the course of this traverse that (Acts 16:6) there was a decision not to preach the word in Asia or in Bithynia, for some reason not really known, but regional hostility possibly had a lot to do with it. The Roman province of Asia was an area generally and intrinsically hostile to their outreach; it possessed a mixture of Greek and Roman deities worship and native Anatolian rites, alongside which Roman emperor-worship was fast developing after the time of Augustus (27 B.C. – A.D. 14). Although geographically near to Galatia, it contrasted strongly since the Galatians were anthropologically different, belonging in origin to a branch of Indo-European Gaulic Celts, some of whom wandered into Europe. In Galatia several languages were spoken: Celtic, Lycaonian, Phrygian and also Anatolian dialects in mountainous areas, but the record shows this sub-region to be the area where the Pauline outreach saw the greatest comparative success before any arrival in West Greece. Now if he naturally supposed a continuing similarity of success to be anticipated along the next part of the route, Paul would receive a bad shock perhaps involving a lengthy period of time spent in struggling with it. The book of Acts gives little of Paul's personal and immediate sufferings, but there is no doubt that many unpleasant things happened to him over the Christian years of his life, a few of which he lists in 2 Corinthians 11: 23-27. Degrees of suffering from physical exposure and from dacoits were very likely frequent across central Asia Minor more than elsewhere, and the time spent fruitlessly in this patch may have amounted to several years. In the slow travel of those days with delays of searching in vain for good ground in which to sow their seed and in the harshness of the rugged mountainous districts of Asia Minor, Paul necessarily took a long time to get as far as entering Europe – which for most of that time might not have been intended as a destination. Also since formed churches are mentioned in parts where success had been achieved, they are likely to have spent considerable time in those parts, perhaps the first third of the tour period. At Acts 15:41 Luke shows Paul confirming churches in Syria and Cilicia without having shown any churches there, but possibly Derbe and Lystra were intended. The account is rather mixed if the note of ordination of elders given as at Derbe and Lystra in Acts 14: 20-23 is unlikely to apply in the earlier time of Paul and Barnabas in their first tour; this ordination is far more tenable in Paul's second visit, the action of substantial church-building in Galatia dating between about late 44 to mid-46. Three years of wearisome and fruitless travel and effort is possible then across Asia Minor coming to arrival at Troas at some time in 49, after which Paul may have spent a year in west Greece prior to coming to Corinth in the South of that country. This period is covered in the narrative of Acts 16:10 to 17:34. Paul's stay at Athens is likely to have been short, if we may estimate from Luke's brevity in the Book of Acts regarding this city, recording only the single occasion where the address on Mars Hill was given. However, some of the Greek intellectuals here are noted to have been interested in the topic of resurrection, "we will hear more of this matter", which suggests some reasonable contact with Paul before he traveled onward to Corinth. In his travels among Greek cities Paul undoubtedly would find a fair degree of familiarity from his younger days back home in Tarsus, where he would have substantial opportunity to converse with local Greeks holding Stoical opinions, and perhaps engaging in debating with them. Contact with intellectual Greeks was not new for him, as a Hellenistic Jew – the short thirteenth of First Corinthians is almost a Stoic poem.

Arriving at Corinth, Paul found himself in the capital of the Roman province of Achaia where dwelt a considerable force of Greek intellect at the location only fifty kilometers from academic Athens. To all intents and purposes Corinth could become a centre in the Greek world from the developing Christian point of view. At the south end of the Lechaion Road and near the propylaea by the agora (city square) in this city an inscription indicating the site of "the synagogue of the Hebrews" has been found. Close by, another such discloses markets: a meat market as noted at 1 Corinthians 10:25 as makellon and another, with Latin inscription as piscario – a fish market. On the South side of the agora was the bema, a large platform elevated up two steps with benches on and around it. It was the public speaking rostrum of construction estimated of date 44, but there is not real evidence that during his eighteen months sojourn here (Acts 18:11) Paul spoke publicly from this bema. Yet as finding acceptance with the Roman representative Gallio (Acts 18: 12-17) he could, and probably did so. Now in 51 the prospect at Corinth was one where not many persons were yet drawn into the Christian faith, but there was certainly potential promise where many among the local Gentiles might become believers. If it may be judged from his letters to Corinth, Paul found a great canvas in this city, for the quality and quantity of those Epistles to the really newly established community not more than about five years old when he was writing. In this connection the note of his preaching by the power of the Holy Spirit at 1 Corinthians 2:4 certainly consisted with the scope and tone of his address made earlier at Athens given in the seventeenth of Acts. It is pleasant to imagine the assertion of speech and preaching not in men's wisdom but in God's power, being delivered to a large but yet unconfirmed crowd, from the central bema, rather than as merely a component inserted in a letter; and it is possible that Paul was thinking back to the time of his oratory at Athens when he wrote it.

Acts 18: 18-23 says that Paul left Corinth after "tarrying there a good while". This departure would be towards the end of the year 51, and also that it took up a journey to Antioch via Ephesus and Caesarea, stopping only briefly in these latter two places. Luke says that he stayed at Antioch "for some time" which may perhaps mean until the Spring of 52, and then indicates that a third tour through the Galatians towns was undertaken. Probably Paul felt concern regarding that Region from whatever news had caused him to remark at Galatians 1.6 "I marvel that ye are so soon removed from him that called you into the grace of Christ unto another Gospel". It is not easy to see any reason for the lapse of some two and a half years between the letter and the new visit here, but such time lapse it seems to have been. Nothing is related about this tour beyond the laconic statement that in the Galatians area he extensively "strengthened all the disciples" (Acts 18:23). After this tour Paul came to Ephesus again where, unlike his visit there for the first time two years. Previously, he now spent a long time whom Acts. 20:31 indicates as three years. This was the period in which he was most energetic and successful in general terms. Very likely signs of a much better prospect in the more purely Greek society along the shores of the Aegean Sea were visible to him when he reached Macedonia for the first time, and this would certainly delay any running back into Galatia urgently, if it is remembered that prior to this arrival the sum total of success in their efforts to evangelize had been meager so recently.

Within what is said in the Corinthians Epistles Paul made three visits to this city, including that of his original arrival in the Spring of 50; in the narrative of Acts Luke does not mention two further visits which would have occurred in the period early 54 to March 57 both made from Ephesus, from which place Paul wrote most of his letters to Corinth in the intervals, predominantly in 54-55 and also the letter to the community at Rome not long afterwards. The Epistle to the Romans was in effect an apologia presenting divine truth by means of using a systematical method, and the existence there of a preponderantly Jewish community at the time is easily inferred from the contents. At Romans 15:24 and 28.

Paul had never anything to do with going to Spain. Here he was saying that he considered the visit he desired and intended to make to them at Rome to be long overdue. At Philemon 9 he styles himself as "Paul the Aged" which normally means at least sixty years of age, thus born around 5 B.C. so even in these days at Ephesus in the fifties he was becoming rather old for much traveling in the conditions for it which then had to be undergone.

Among the several river valleys on the deeply indented west coast of Asia Minor the part of the coast where the Meander River reached the Aegean Sea gave the best situation for a port-city, and here Ephesus became an important commercial and religious centre in the Graeco-Roman world, as the capital of the Roman province of Asia. This is not evident in later times, because over the centuries the natural harbour here was gradually silted up by a nearer and smaller river, the Cayster, and the city became an inland one to the extent of about seven kilometers. Archaeological work has confirmed the existence of a significant pagan temple to Artemis at Ephesus which had been built in the sixth and rebuilt in the third century B.C., it has also uncovered a circular amphitheatre at the east end of the stadium where gladiatorial and wild animal contests and combats took place. By an inscription here the stadium was rebuilt in the reign of Nero (54-68), and from 1 Corinthians 15:32 there is little doubt that Paul was at some time involved in some of the amphitheatre combat, and close to that time of the rebuilding. The reference in Acts 19: 27-35 to Diana of the Ephesians is just the Roman form for the Greek Artemis, where this part of the narration testifies

Paul in a Jerusalem Street
Acts. 21:31-33

to the contemporary strength of pagan opposition which the Christians were up against. Nothing is known of a Christian community at Ephesus before Paul went there, but the text at Acts. 18: 19-21 shows that he found a promising prospect for evangelical outreach to which he might certainly return at a more propitious time in the close future. Acts 19 gives a record of numerous happenings with Paul in this city, but many more things than are written of appears certain in the considerable time of three years with a man as active as this in the volatile environment.

Near the end of 56 Paul departed from Ephesus for West Greece, spending some three months there (Acts 20:3) and was at Philippi in Macedonia at the time of a Passover of unleavened bread (20:6) that is, in March 57. After a few weeks at Troas on the Asia coast Paul traveled twenty kilometers overland to meet the ship at Assos, then took a three days voyage to Miletus on the same coast (Acts 20:14-15). In his intention to reach Jerusalem in time for the annual celebration of Pentecost (20:16) in the month of June, this could only just be done and with some urgency as it would already be late April, and the bringing of brethren sixty kilometers from Ephesus to meet him at Miletus (Acts 20:17-18) would take time. There was then a voyage from Miletus to Caesarea taking about nine days, and he remained at Caesarea for about five days (21:10). Then some two days of travel by road to Jerusalem brings the journey time from Miletus to Jerusalem to sixteen days, so perhaps Paul departed from Miletus in mid-May 57.

A week after arriving in Jerusalem a Jewish riot broke out (Acts 21:27) and Paul was arrested. Subsequently he was taken under Roman guard to Caesarea (23:23-30) and held for two years (24:27) under two procurators: firstly Felix and then Festus, and finally underwent a voyage to Rome which seems to have begun in about June 59. Closely described in Acts 27:1 to 28:14 this voyage would have taken three months (Acts 28:11) plus one week (28:14). giving the arrival at Rome of approximate date October 59; Acts

27:12 indicates the season of winter and 28:11 gives a further duration of three months.

As coming into Roman hands the Apostle was held only for his own protection since there was no visible charge against him under Roman law; and Paul could, and did, claim common tort as a Roman citizen (Acts 22:25-30). As with Pontius Pilate in the trial of Jesus, the Roman authority could neither convict Paul as a prisoner nor understand the hostility of the Jewish mob causing him into their notice. The prisoner answered well, the plaintiffs were dismissed, and the procurator Felix held Paul for further access, having no idea as to what else to do. In the text at Acts 24:24-26 there is no credence that Paul attempted to evangelize or to furnish a bribe for release. He was now held down to the end of Felix's tour of duty and the successor Festus, as being a man of more action, quickly brought a fresh hearing in the Jews

Paul Before Festus
Acts. 25:6-12

v. Paul problem. This was followed up by opening the case before the local vassal king Herod Agrippa at Caesarea (Acts 25:13) in which Porcius Festus and Herod Agrippa would be well aware that Paul, as prisoner of the "powers that be", was nothing to do with the familiar everyday rabble which they controlled. Agrippa now aged about 31 generally aligned himself with Roman rather than Jewish interests, and was interested in the case because Paul had appealed unto Caesar (Acts 25:11). In this royal audience no Jewish interest was present. If the speech given at Acts 26: 2-8 is correct verbatim it might be attributed to a working in the principle of Mark 13:11, an unction of the Holy Spirit attending divine guidance upon Paul: it is a speech of plain statements with no flattery or any fear of those in high position, but rendering honour where due and avoiding any critique of opposers. Additionally however, Acts 26: 9-23 is likely spurious, as a glaring padding of colour superfluously supplied. The shout of Festus follows from Paul's inviting question, "Why should it be beyond the belief of men such as yourselves that God should raise the dead?" The pagan Roman rejected the Christian connection with resurrection, but the Roman Jew Agrippa seems to have been set thinking seriously upon it.

Paul's removal to Rome was undertaken of necessity and Luke, whose close detail of the voyage (plus Colossians 4:14) suggests this author of Acts being present, rendered the narrative meager. Paul's legal appeal must involve a hearing, probably before a Senate Committee, but the verses in Acts 28: 16-22 do not in any way cover it. Presumably the Jewish interests drifted away, and Paul was able to get to work "with all confidence, no man forbidding him" suggests Luke left Rome in late 61 or early 62. It is widely believed that Luke drafted a work from units of information about Jesus' ministry, designated as Proto-Luke, and there are several factors pointing to this. If affirmative it would be undertaken at Rome in those quiet years of 60-61; the Preface to his eventual gospel account at Luke 1: 1-4 belongs to his pre-Mark draft originally, and in the other Preface at Acts 1:1-3 "The former treatise" almost certainly refers to the draft Proto-Luke. There are indications that the draft and Acts were written not very long apart in time. "Theophilus" in the Prefaces may be a general Reader address as meaning "Lover of God", rather than a specific individual naming.

6
The Whereabouts of Other Prominent Christians Before 60

Whereas the Book of Acts says a great deal about St. Paul, it gives far less of Simon Peter who appears in Chapters 1, 2, 4 and 5 but mainly in the account of his coastal activities at Caesarea and Joppa in Acts 9: 32-11:18. The Apostle Phillip is noted with limited traveling from Jerusalem to Samaria, Gaza and the Coast in Acts 8:5-13 and 8:26-40, but John is hardly seen at all except as working with Simon Peter in the earliest days. He seems to have been at Jerusalem until the early forties. His brother James Zebedee was killed by the sword (Acts 12:2) perhaps not long before Herod Antipas, who caused this murder, met his own death which is known from secular sources to have occurred in the year 44; by Acts 12:19 Herod was still alive after James' departure from this life. James the Less or, the Just, became head of the Jewish Church at Jerusalem, although there is an impression from the first few Chapters of Acts that Simon Peter assumed a degree of leadership at the beginning. James is always mentioned only at Jerusalem, as for instance by Paul in Galatians 1:19 and 2:9 and noted in Acts 15:13 and 21:18 – he is never seen elsewhere, and certainly died there. Of others of the original apostolate of Twelve, nothing is given in the canon. The best probability is that, under a commission of Jesus for them to travel outward without ultimate limit as indicated at the end of the gospel accounts, they undertook to do so at various starting times and in different directions, James opting to remain and lead what was then the Mother Church. Evidently St. Luke had no source material in regard to most of their business upon the Lord's commission.

With Simon Peter there was a "watershed" formed on a difference made by the point of his decision to tour on the Palestine coast, prior to this he had been working together with John but thereafter worked alone, in the strictly apostolic sense Acts 12: 3-16 confirms that he was in Jerusalem when James Zebedee was murdered and, like Paul and Silas later at Philippi he was liberated from an imprisonment by one or more friendly guards. On being released he repaired the house of John Mark's mother in Jerusalem (Acts 12:12) which they were using. It is likely to be the house of the Last Supper with its upper room of Mark 14: 13-17, since the group forming Jesus' ministry were outsiders relative to this city and so had few possibilities of accommodation within its walls. In this district Jesus had normally stopped in Bethany village nearby, and no other house is known for them actually in Jerusalem before the commissioning for the last supper. Luke says that after greeting the people at this Jerusalem house Simon Peter departed "and went into another place", obviously to get away from the current circumstances of Herod's hostility focused against the leading Apostles who were yet ready to hand. He needed to get away altogether, and the pressure in this is confirmed by the note at Acts 12:18-19 that Herod had the prison guards executed. While nothing is said of Simon Peter's destination on leaving Jerusalem almost certainly for the last time, it seems certain to have been Antioch. In this part of the Book of Acts. Luke was not chronological, but took the subject for narrative in blocks, here jumping back from Jerusalem in 43-44 with Herod by some two years to the large matter of Barnabas and Saul setting out on their primary tour early in 42. If the birth date of Simon Peter is reasonably guessed as about 10 B.C. in which case he would be about forty-two years of age when, as the older man he was outrun by John in their race to the empty tomb in 33 (John 20: 3-4), he would already be in his fifties when going to Antioch. He may have been elder by a few years in the apostolate, which would give him an apparent significance seen particularly in the St. Matthew gospel – though not in the direct witness of that of St. John. The Gospel according to St. Matthew may have been written at Antioch and was certainly written in the last two decades of the first century A.D. when a rift between Jews and Christians had seriously developed and the St. Matthew author intended his project to aid the ailing Jewish Christian following.

In the first half of the forties there was a rapid growth of the Christian community at Antioch to some extent due to St. Barnabas but also perhaps later to an addition of the authority and work of Simon Peter. This city became a central home base outside of St. Paul's work, and even Paul reported back there after finally departing from Corinth (Acts 18: 18-23). From the little we know of Simon Peter, "newly risen" and faithfully eager after the Lord's reappearances with forgiveness over the denials, and Barnabas the "son of encouragement" who as an ex-Levite had given all he materially possessed to the gathered community, it seems certain that these men if associated at Antioch variously across the fifties would work well together. Barnabas' nephew John Mark furnishes a link between them because, as most scholars now agree, Mark was associated with Simon Peter in the project of writing the earliest gospel. By the narrative in the eleventh of Acts Saul or Paul was very likely unaware of Simon Peter's work on the Coast involving a new outreach to Gentiles, as it was only after Simon Peter's report of it that Saul was brought to Antioch, not Jerusalem - into circulation by Barnabas; therefore he was likely to be taken aback on discovering Simon's regular accommodation of Gentiles at Antioch, to which he refers in Galatians 2: 11-16. It seems remarkable that in his letters Paul did not give credit where it was due to both Barnabas and Simon Peter.

In the absence of any further note of Simon Peter or of any more travels by him, it is only possible to conjecture that he remained as certainly a Church father at Antioch and probably died there, perhaps in the mid or later sixties. The writer of the St. Matthew gospel, about whom nothing is definitely known, may either have known Simon personally or have been associated with others who did. If done in the eighties this writing dates only about thirty years after the Apostle's time, perhaps less, thus the older and younger man would be largely contemporary, with an overlap of years in the same location. From the letters of St. Ignatius written in 114 it is clear that the office of bishop was established earlier at Antioch; also Ignatius included what seems to have been dealing from first-hand knowledge of Simon Peter's teaching to the extent of that community having still a direct remembrance of him. A few verses in the Gospel according to St. Matthew show unmistakable signs of church influence in the sources on which the St. Matthew author depended, as at Matthew 16: 16-19 with Simon Peter singled out – according to this account – as a foundation of institutional Church with keys of binding and loosing. There is neither indication of such institutional thing having been a concern of the Lord Jesus throughout His ministry, which must show substantially if it had been, nor any sign that Mark or especially John knew anything about it, the former writing earlier than the St. Matthew author and the latter later. When Simon Peter himself came to write his General Epistle the address at 1 Peter 1:1 "to the strangers" in many parts of Asia Minor strongly suggests that he was well aware of the work of others, but had not traveled in those parts himself. As this Epistle contains no reference to Paul, it is virtually certain that it was intended for districts such as Pontus, Cappadocia and Bithynia which lay outside of Paul's travel routes. There is a good likelihood that missionary efforts of outreach in those areas were working out of Antioch; 1 Peter 5:13 includes a greeting to the recipients from Mark, so evidently they knew him. Already in these days of the forties the Christian outreach consisted in several distinct branches: Jerusalem originally and now Antioch, plus St. Paul out on the road on really his own account; the leaders in these were thus James the Just, Simon Peter probably in unison with Barnabas, and Paul. From the later Ignatius the particular theology of the doctrine developing at Antioch and in some ways differing from Paul (but without contradiction) appears to have been Petrine, closer to James than to Paul, a teaching model reflected in First Peter. It also carries detectable doctrinal and literal coincidences or concordances with Mark.

We have next to look at several prominent Christians who associated and worked with Paul: Apollos, Aquila and Priscilla, and Timotheus. At Acts 18:24-19:1 Luke gives an unusually comprehensive note about Apollos, contrasting with his regular limitation to little more than names in the cases of other co-workers with Paul such as Silas or Timotheus; Titus, whom Paul mentions in his letters, is not mentioned in Acts at all. By this account Apollos was an Alexandrian Jew blessed with a sound education and said to have been baptized by John the Baptist, where Luke says that he "knew" this baptism. Where Acts 18: 26b says that Aquila and Priscilla, whom Paul had recently brought to Ephesus from Corinth before moving on, "expounded unto Apollos the way of God more perfectly", possibly the real meaning here is simply that they persuaded him, and certainly made him welcome, into joining St. Paul's band. It is surely confirmed by the next verse where Apollos was given a letter of introduction to apply at Corinth. As originally diaspora Jews from Pontus (northern Asia Minor along the Black Sea) Aquila and his wife Prisicilla are first noted at Acts 18: 2-3 as having come from Rome as enforced exiles, to Corinth; here Luke mentions that both Aquila and Paul were tentmakers by trade, and "wrought together" at Corinth. In 2 Corinthians 8: 1-10 Paul seems to have given the church only advice (verse 10) materially, but it is likely that he sometimes earned for his own sustaining (vide 1 Cor. 4:12 and 2 Cor. 11: 8-9) and perhaps gave contributions to the church from his own earnings. This couple then went with Paul to Ephesus where they remained, being with Paul there later when he was writing to Corinth and signing off one of the letters with salutations from various associates at Ephesus: "Aquilla and Priscilla salute you much in the Lord, with the church that is in their house. "Since both names Aquilla and Priscilla are Latin, it is possible that they had Roman connections, but not certain that they were Jews by nationality; if expelled from Rome under the Claudius Edict of 49 this could apply to Christians, because Rome then identified these believers as Jews irrespectively. In such case a first reason for Paul to make contact with them on his arriving at Corinth would be religious rather than in the tent making interest. Paul's view of them as teachers in 1 Cor. 12:28 suggests that their faith had not originally depended on their meeting him. By Romans 16: 3-4 Aquilla and Priscilla had at some time risked their lives in Paul's behalf during one of the dangers faced at Ephesus; but they seem to have remained in this place, and were still there when Barnabas wrote to Timothy in about 65 (2 Tim. 4:19). Clearly the rolls of names here of Paul's intimacy belong to Ephesus, not Rome; and the addition of it beyond the final prayer at Romans 15: 31-33 would form an odd postscript.

Apollos was still with Paul at Ephesus (1 Cor. 16:12) as being his own man: "As touching our brother Apollos, I greatly desired him to come to you with the brethren; but his will was not at all to come at this time, but he will come when he shall have convenient time". Apollos would revisit Corinth when he was ready. At 1 Cor. 3: 5-6 Paul ranks Apollos with himself in what, from 1 Corinthians 1:12 seems to have been a local environment of emerging loyalty cliques: from Acts 18: 28 certainly Apollos was able to impressively make his mark. Paul may have suffered from some sensitivity in regard to the Corinthians laudation of Apollos, a possibility suggested by the text of 1 Cor. 4:15b-17a: "Ye have not many fathers; for in Christ Jesus I have begotten you through the gospel. Wherefore I beseech you, be ye followers of me. For this cause I have sent unto you Timotheus". The great and most famous missionary Apostle was an educated man certainly, but he could not match the use of philosophical eloquence applied by Apollos; it shows up in Paul's human referencing as being "rude in speech, but not a whit behind the very chiefest Apostles" (2 Cor. 11:6 and 5), and at 2 Cor. 3:1 where he asks, "Did I need any letters of recommendations to you?" undoubtedly referring to such thing furnished for Apollos (Acts 18:27). In the light of all this it may well be, that a main reason for Apollos' refusal to go again to Corinth just yet was of seeking no unwelcome resurgence of partisan stress. Without more evidence it is presumed that Apollos came from Alexandria to Ephesus in 52 while Paul was away touring in the Galatian districts prior to settling for some time at Ephesus. His acquaintance with Christian doctrine as referred at Acts 18:25 clearly did not come through Paul; in the Greek he taught *ta peri tou* 'Ihisou "the things concerning Jesus", but the English translators only repeated "of the world" from Kyrie: "the way of the Lord" and then again "the things of the Lord" in this same verse Acts 18:25. The construing is important, and it is good to consider Martin Luther's suggestion that Apollos is the best candidate supplying a name for the unknown author of the Book of Hebrews.

There is no indication as to when or under what circumstances Apollos first left Corinth to go to Ephesus. Considering the obvious significance of this man the record is unsatisfactory; but the co-worker Timotheus is far more frequently noticed, especially by Paul. In the Book of Acts we first meet him at the Galatian town of Lystra (16: 1-3) as a son of mixed parcentage, a young man now adult in the mid-forties to whom Paul gave preferment to include him henceforth in his entourage. Timotheus then traveled with Paul and Silas on this continuing tour, though in the substantial narration in the sixteenth of Acts about vicissitudes at Philippi his name does not appear therein alongside those of Paul and Silas. Further along the journey however, he remained at Corinth after arriving at this place with Paul from Athens, but nothing more is noted of him by this form of his name used by Luke. It is generally agreed that Silas is identical with Silvanus, which appears with Paul at 1 Thessalonians 1:1 and with Simon Peter at 1 Peter 5:12.

Clearly remaining with Paul in the move to Ephesus, Timotheus was sent from there back into Macedonia (Acts 19:22) and seems to have worked there down to the time when Paul made another tour through West Greece (Acts 20: 1-4). Although many details are not given, probably Timotheus remained with Paul for the rest of their days, because the greeting at Philippians 1:1 shows that he was with Paul in Rome, this in the early sixties. In the various points in Paul's letters where Timotheus is mentioned (1 Thessalonians 1:1, 3:2, 1 Corinthians 4:17), (2 Corinthians 1:19 and at the start of Philippians and Colossians) he is evidently a trusted associate. By Romans 16:21 he was with Paul at Ephesus when the Epistle to the Romans was written before the journey to Jerusalem. A major reason for Timotheus being sent to Macedonia specifically and perhaps in the year 55 was, that news had been received of peresecution at Thessalonika. Paul was concerned over this and sought to offer them encouragement, and it is significant that he applied Timotheus in the task instead of going to them himself; but Timotheus was able to bring back good news regarding that community. In 1 Corinthians 4: 1-17, a text which appears to have been in his second letter to Corinth, Paul felt a need to recommend Timotheus as a worthy representative, and here Timotheus appears to have been the bearer of that current letter from Ephesus. Possibly Paul anticipated that they might complain that he himself was not then visiting, but sending a substitute. Thus he was urging the brethren at Corinth to put Timotheus at his ease as may seem necessary and to send him back in peace as one equally engaged serving the Lord as they understood the work in hand to be. If there were difficulties here unresolved, this would explain why Titus subsequently features in the Corinth correspondence and not Timotheus. Further, in the later letters presented together as Second Corinthians most of the few references to Titus are now found, so it looks as if Timotheus came to a point where he could no longer serve as a deputy for Paul at Corinth. In later years it is evident that Paul was able to send him from Rome to Philippi (Philippians 2:19) at least as an intention, to bring back a report on the wellbeing of that community as one genuinely anxious for their welfare – if there was any difficulty, it was reserved to Corinth.

By 2 Corinthians 7:6 Titus, who first appears at Antioch according to what Paul says at Galatians 2: 1-3 about activities in the early forties, had been to Corinth after the last visit there of Timotheus, and the result of his sojourn had been to cheer Paul up sufficiently to half apologize for his previous letter which (1 Corinthians 4: 6-8) had railed at them as being "puffed-up". Perhaps a supposed deficiency in the character conduct of the brethren at Corinth was merely Paul's personal opinion, that Titus had found no substance in it, from which Paul in 2 Corinthians 7:9 wrote to tell them that he rejoiced in that they now "sorrowed" to repentance"! The references to Titus int 2 Corinthians 8:6 and 8:23 do not add anything thus far, and at 12:18 ibid. the mention comes chronologically earlier than the time of Titus returning to Paul with a clearing report applied in a letter referred in 2 Corinthians 2: 3-4 and 7:12. There are indications that Titus later worked with Barnabas, whom Luke only notes in Acts 15:39 as having taken his nephew Mark in leaving Antioch for Cyprus, giving nothing more of these men in Acts the choice of Cyprus as a destination in 44 may have been influenced by the fact of Barnabas having previously lived there when he practiced as a Levite (Acts 4:36), but they may have wished to return to the scenes recently visited, now without Paul, as a fresh opportunity. Nothing more is recorded about Barnabas down to the beginning of the sixties, but on the basis of the note about this Apostle's connection with is protégé Timothy remarked here in Chapter 5 we may catch up with him through the Pastoral Epistles to Titus and Timothy.

7
The Sixties

The General Epistle of James was written as a document for the Jewish Church and not least, to accommodate Jewish converts to Christianity, in about 59 or 60, As largely specific towards their ethnic purposes this letter remained unaccepted, although evidently known to Clement of Rome in the nineties, until well into the third century beyond doubts held early then by Origen regarding a canon status for it. This Epistle was unlikely to be much known among the Gentile Christian communities to whom it was not sent, yet Clement to the Corinthians and Ignatius to Ephesus in 114 both quoted from it. The document, less replete with the high doctrines than are the letters of Paul, Barnabas, Simon Peter and John, passed through severe scrutiny by the Church fathers before it could be eventually universally received; but in James the ground principles of Christianity are taken for granted, and the work seems to have been only limited to a special design of counteracting drift tendencies within the community of the Jews but without much thinking about the Gentiles. With this work of James we have already a contemporary awareness of clouds moving up on the Christian horizon immediately after the fifties, which were soon to gather over the Gentile communities as well.

At Mark 6:3 James is listed as being among the brothers of the Lord Jesus, but this is not literal. Among the Ancients it was a custom to use the term "brother" generally for more remote kinsmen such as cousins or male relatives-in-law, and this was long continued – even in pre-modern English "brother-German" meant cousin. From the hypomnemata of Hegesippus, Greek fragments quoted by Eusebius in the fourth century Joseph and Cleophas (Luke 1:27 and 24:18) appear to have been actual full brothers, Cleophas identical with Alphaeus (Mark 3:18) being the father of James and Jude. Then these boys would be associated with the Holy family only as reckoned to be cousins by Joseph as Jesus' assumed father: it could be but a loose in-law relationship and without blood connection. Clearly the mother of James was Mary Cleophas indicated by John 19:25 as being present at the cross: in the roll of women named at the cross that given in this verse as Jesus' mother's sister was Salome Zebedee of Mark 15:40 where Mary the mother of James is certainly Mary Cleophas. There is then no question of James being a brother of Jesus through either Mary the Virgin or Joseph, so the basis of James' authority position at Jerusalem could not derive directly from any special family relationship with Jesus, overtopping others; indeed the relationship of the Zebedee brothers as sons of Salome, a sister of the Virgin, was closer to Jesus as first cousins. In their new bond of faith adherence the Apostles at Jerusalem either left James free to volunteer for the responsibility or else chose him, to officiate. It is unclear as to how far James believed, with others, that their mission to the Jews would pave the way for Gentile Christianity, dating at least from the conference on circumcision.

There are two separate accounts recording the death of James at Jerusalem: one by Josephus writing in the nineties of the first century, the other by Hegeisippus writing in about 155. In "Antiquities of the Jews" Book 20.9.1 Josephus says that the Sadducee high priest Ananus seized an opportunity when the procurator had died suddenly: "Festus was now dead, and Albinus was but upon the road; so he assembled the Sanhedrim of the judges, and brought before them the brother of Jesus, who was called Christ, whose name was James, and some others; and when he had formed an accusation against them as breakers of the law, he delivered them to be stoned". It was a lynching become possible in a short period of absence of Roman control, between the loss of one procurator and the hurried arrival of his successor, dating between April and July 62; not normally possible, because the Jews had no authority to pass death sentence nor carry it out, in Roman Palestine. Hegesippus says that James was killed after being presented to the people at Passover time, when he proclaimed Jesus as the Son of man seated at God's right hand. According to this narration James was then cast down, stoned, and clubbed to death. Of these two accounts the former (from another faith) may be reckoned as more reliable than that of Hegesippus the Christian Jew.

Like James, and with another General Epistle closely contemporary with him, Simon Peter was concerned in regard to a perceived need to publish a form of strengthening the general practice of faith belief; but unlike James his concern was with Gentile converts, not Jewish Christians. Firstly, let us run a similar exercise as with St. Paul, in drawing from the document the parts which assemble as its universal acme.

"Blessed be the God and Father of our Lord Jesus Christ, which according to His abundant mercy hath begotten us again unto a living hope by the resurrection of Jesus Christ from the dead, to an inheritance incorruptible and undefiled, and that fadeth not away, reserved in heaven for you who are kept by the power of God through faith unto salvation, ready to be revealed in the last time.

Unto whom it was revealed that not unto themselves, but unto us, they did minister the things which are now reported unto you by them that have preached the gospel unto you, with the Holy Ghost sent down from heaven; which things the angels desire to look into.

For as much as ye know that ye were not redeemed with corruptible things such as silver and gold, from your vain conversation by tradition from your fathers but with the precious blood of Christ, as of a lamb without blemish and without spot, who verily was fore ordained before the foundation of the world, but was manifest in these last times for you who, by Him, do believe in God, that raised Him up from the dead and gave Him glory: that your faith and hope might be in God. That ye are born again: not of corruptible seed, but of incorruptible, by the Word of God which liveth and abideth for ever. For all flesh is as grass, and all the glory of man as the flower of grass. The grass withereth, and the flower thereof falleth away; but the Word of the Lord endureth for ever. And this is the word which by the gospel is preached unto you.

But ye are a chosen generation, a royal priesthood, a holy nation, a peculiar people; that ye should show forth the praises of Him who hath called you out of darkness into His marvelous light. Ye in time past were not a people, but are now the people of God: which had not obtained mercy, but now have obtained mercy. For even hereunto were ye called; because Christ also suffered for us, leaving us an example, that ye should follow His steps: who did no sin, neither was guile found in His mouth. Who, when He was reviled, reviled not again; when He suffered, He threatened not, but committed Himself to Him that judgeth righteously. Who His own self bare our sins in His own body on the tree that we, being dead to sins, should live unto righteousness: by Whose stripes ye were healed. For ye were as sheep going astray, but are now returned unto the shepherd of your souls.

For we have not followed cunningly devised fables, when we made known unto you the power and coming of our Lord Jesus Christ, but were eyewitnesses of His majesty. For He received from God the father honour and glory, when there came such a voice of Him from the excellent glory, This is my beloved Son , in whom I am well pleased. And this voice which came from heaven we heard, when we were with Him in the holy mount we have also a more sure word of prophecy, whereunto ye do well that ye take heed, as unto a light that shineth in a dark place until the day dawn, and the day star arise in your hearts: knowing this first, that the prophecy in old time came not by the will of man; but holy men of God spoke as they were moved by the Holy Ghost.

But the God of all grace, who hath called us unto His eternal glory by Christ Jesus, after that ye have suffered awhile make you perfect, stablish, strengthen, settle you. To him be glory and dominion for ever and ever. Amen".

1 Peter 1: 3-5, 1:12, 1:18-21, 1:23-25, 2;9-10, 2:21-25 and 2 Peter 1: 16-23).

The final reference here is given from Second Peter as it is familiarly presented; but the Epistle should really be taken as one only, the Epistle of Peter comprising Six chapters as including "Second Peter 1" because the second and third of second Peter is a writing of the mid-second century by somebody else, a churchman concerned with lapses of that time which had by then emerged true on the prophecies long before laid out in the Epistle of St. Jude. The note disclosing Paul's Epistles as already collected for the Church (2 Peter 3:16) could not have been written by Simon Peter in the mid-first century. In the aspect of literary analysis the first Chapter of Second Peter is an undivided part-and-parcel with the fifth of First Peter, flowing together but totally unconnected with 2 Peter 2 and 3 in either subject or syntax. From 1 Peter 5:10 directly to 2 Peter1:3ff and then finishing with 1 Peter 5:11 we have: "But the God of all grace, who hath made you perfect, stablish, strengthen and settle you – According as His divine power hath given unto us all things that pertain unto life and godliness, through the knowledge of Him that hath called us to glory and virtue" in 2 Peter 1:4-1:21 is the whole body of an amplification with behavioral specifics on the general advising given along the Chapter 1 Peter 5; then finally, 2 Peter 1:21 back into the original signing-off – "For the prophecy came in old time not by the will of man, but holy men o f God spake as they were moved by the Holy Ghost. – to Him be glory and dominion for ever and ever. Amen".

The Sixties

In this closing of what is really the Epistle of Simon Peter the actual writing is stated to be done by Silvanus (Silas, with Luke), virtually certain to be back at Antioch now in 60 or 61, and Mark was with them at the time. At 1 Peter 5:13 we have another glaring translation error, because no elected church then existed at Babylon. The term *babulownia* in the Greek applies in "a confusion of tongues"; Simon Peter was acknowledging the fact of numerous languages now in the Christendom of the Gentiles, already spread as they were into many lands, "Salutation to you, whatever your language." Possibly the Greek term may have derived from the ancient Tower of Babel idea which appears in the Book of Genesis. In the address beginning First Peter the reference is to people living in a large stretch of country along the south shore of the Black Sea where obviously some outreach had been made in, perhaps throughout, the fifties other than by St. Paul "Marcus my son salutes you" (1 Peter 5:13) – possibly Barnabas and Mark had been involved with this Region, working out of Antioch. But it is possible only to conjecture in the absence of anything better in definite records to lead to other hypothesis on a sounder basis; as with the gospel reports (vide John 20:30)so also throughout the New Testament many things which had happened and were important for us to know, were simply not recorded.

Taking this Epistle as a whole in the intention of the project, Simon Peter was looking back strongly to the Passion and Resurrection events of less than thirty years previously, and to the ancient prophecies concerning them, view expressed "in a nutshell" at 1 Peter 2: 24-25 recalling Jesus in that whole joined connection, Him crucified and our stripes healed by it, on the text of Isaiah 53: 5-6 where the text as presented gives Bishop superficially after Shepherd it is probably a spurious church addition, although this office did originate at Antioch; but against this, the prospect of an insertion is rendered less likely by the fact of a similar early appearance of the Episcopal term in Titus 1:7 within two years of the Peter Epistle. But in particular there is a strong impression that the writing was, at least in part, motivated by thoughts for the future time in a realization that the witnesses who filled the early days were inevitably dying out. Already nearly a generation after the great events of the thirties they must have seen that the close post-resurrection euphoria had cooled; and they knew that younger people were coming up, but had not experienced that phenomena at first-hand. Simon Peter shows his concern in this at 2 Peter 1:12-15 where he desires to put all Christians in remembrance after his own decease, "knowing that shortly I must put off this my tabernacle". The same thing is found with Barnabas at 2 Timothy 4:6: "For I am now ready to be offered, and the time of my departure is at hand", exhorting Timothy in the previous verse to do the work of an evangelist for the future. This was written in about 65 when he yet had at least two years given him, but the principle of Apostles in the first-hand knowledge providing an accommodation for others in the future remains.

At the opening of First Peter the writer does not use his original appellation of Simon (by contrast it does appear in the externally added opening verse of Second Peter, which suggests that he was in his time generally known simply as Peter – though it may have been retained in the Aramaic form of Kephas and merely translated later by the Greeks in the course of making copies. Mark 1:16 gives the original name as Simon at the time of the calling of the four earliest disciples, then gives at Mark 2:15 "And Simon He surnamed Peter"; St. John recalling the events from personal memory says at John 1:42 that the Lord Jesus gave this name at the Calling: "Thou shalt be called Kephas". In 1 Corinthians 1:12 Paul used the Aramaic form; but where the verse in John includes an English insertion "which is by interpretation, a stone", there is doubt about this rendering which for the Greek would then be lithos, not petrus, a rock. In the Hebraic family of language to which Aramaic belongs, the vocabulary is limited to some six thousand words only in the Hebrew, and often the meaning must be taken from the context in which the word is used. Here we have at least five meanings with Kephas; and to style Simon as "the rock" would not be a simple description of this character as deduced from the gospels where he appears impulsively volatile to the extent of a liability to failure – and the giving of an appellation was a solemn act of some significance. Among the various meanings in the Aramaic we have "arisen", "stood up", "Came into being", "came to pass", and "stood firm", so the best likelihood here seems to be "newly arisen, to develop to the full" as would apply for instance to a rising of the moon, which does describe that part of Simon's Christian career which is known. It is remotely possible that the source for the St. Mathew author confused it in the Greek ek klesis "of a calling apart" for Church, and a tying up of Simon's name Kephas with the church became subsequently garbled; because to Jesus, Who conferred the name, the Christian group which was in any case only afterwards so designated consists in a body of the loyal people of God centred in Him (as is most clear in First Peter), in view of the kingdom of heaven and not a militant clique of the world.

At the beginning of the sixties Simon was writing to people whom he seems to indicate as "strangers", which suggests he had not been among them personally, but clearly a good deal of information about them had been brought back to him. From what he says, many were converts from paganism, i.e. "Once you were not a religious people, but now you are a people of God" (1 Peter 2:10), while others were undoubtedly of a class or caste known as God-fearers, that is people along the fringe of monotheistic Judaism as proselytes but not fully accepted by the Jews, people who had some acquaintance with scripture: "Unto them which be disobedient, the stone which the builders disallowed, the same is made the head of the corner" (1 Peter 2:17 quoting Psalm 118:22). Where a person having been put into a job without much ability for it yet improves in the course of doing it and in being given this chance then notably succeeds, which is called in modern parlance "The Peter Principle", this was certainly true with the original Peter. That which had puzzled him back in the twenties as for instance reported at Mark 10:23

and Matthew 19:27 when he asked what might be the reward in store for the disciples having given up everything to follow Jesus, no longer confused him in the sixties when he was readily able to give general and universal assurance of an incorruptible and undying inheritance through the re-begetting unto a living hope by the resurrection of Jesus Christ from the dead. Certainly the Christian must be aware that years are required to learn the deep truths of this faith, and in his own words here Peter saw that others would firstly be "as newborn babes, desiring the sincere milk of the word, that they may grow thereby"(1 Peter 2.2). In the practical advice portions of his excellent Epistle he enjoins that the believer who has attained the Christian hope should be always ready to give an answer regarding it when asked: not to be forward in thrusting it at others without enquiry. This practicality shines more brightly still in the final part of the General Epistle: "Giving all diligence, add to your faith virtue, and to virtue knowledge; and to knowledge temperance, to temperance patience, and to patience godliness; and to godliness brotherly kindness, and to brotherly kindness charity". This chain of graces forms a complete whole, and its links are in first-class order, in beginning with virtue which , carrying faith into action, is the grace of doing; knowledge meant here is the practical wisdom of distinguishing between what is real and what is false, for action engaging a holding back in temperate self-control and a holding on in patience. This section of the chain is concerned with the management of ourselves, but then the closing group godliness, brotherly kindness and charity supplies the positive aspect of relations to God, to fellow Christians and to all mankind. Starting with faith and ending with love this chain has no need to include the common virtues such as honesty and truthfulness, which it already covers. Where the term add to your faith is given in the English it comes rather from a term in the Greek from ancient theatre implying "to furnish a chorus" – this may fairly be taken as a scale of graces essential for harmony.

In general Simon Peter was, like Paul, writing for the present, although certainly he felt some concern that the Christian work should go on after his time, expressing an interest in "stirring them up by putting them in remembrance" before he must "shortly put off this tabernacle;" but it is very unlikely he would have been able to conjecture any possibility of people learning beneficially from him two thousand years beyond his own time. But, we do. According to the gospel accounts he had sinned with lying denials even after Jesus had said in his personal connection on one occasion, "Get thee behind Me, Satan; for thou savourest the things of men, not of God". Yet the next twenty-five years of immersion in faith belief transformed him such that, in reading "between the lines" we learn from Simon that it is possible to be polished by the dust of one's own old sins, just as a stone is polished on its own dust until a water test will show the polish to be genuine if unchanged wet and dry. Simon Peter has furnished a clear example, in his own person even in the limited extent of our knowledge of him from the meagre records, of how an imperfect but warmhearted and impulsive man may be improved by opportunity and training with discipline functioning through hardship, to become an instrument of God in the purposes of Love. It is a fruitful prospect. According to Mark 16:7 Simon Peter is named as being given special invitation in the news of Jesus' rising; this was a typical dispensation of the Lord's grace after the Petrine denials: meeting a special need in the disciple who was aghast at his own deeply personal regression and had wept. Additionally Luke 24:34 says that in the reappearance Jesus had appeared to Simon before revisiting the others. This Apostle knew that his sinning – as of simply an average man – was together forgiven in that the Lord had borne punishment for him.

In the two Epistles James and First Peter there are parallels clearly visible, thus: flesh and grass wither away (1 Peter 1:24 and James 1:10-11); a crown of life received (1 Peter 5:4 and James 1:12); an injunction to abstain from lusts (1 Peter 2:11 and James 1:14-16); quality of governing the tongue (1 Peter 3:10 and James

3:3-12); true prayers are answered (1 Peter 3:12 and James 5:16); no harm comes to the follower of God (1 Peter 3:13 and James 4:7); charity covers a multitude of sins (1 Peter 4:8 and James 5:20); God resists the proud (1 Peter 5:5 and James 4:6); humble yourselves that God may exalt you in due time (1 Peter 5:15 and James 4:10); and, all perfect giving is from above (2) Peter 1:3 and James 1:7-18). It summarizes the style of their interpretation carrying forward the mass of traditional units of Christian belief across the previous two decades as an interpretation applied in experience which told them things were slowly changing, an inevitability in the world of flux where all things are indeed temporal. The guidance given by these first luminaries was valid for those who were intended to receive it, and it is equally valid for us; they met the future perhaps better than they knew or hoped, and in meeting human spiritual needs their ladders reach further into the well of this world's sinning state. Within the portion of the given equipment of faith apparatus James means comparatively less to us, but Simon Peter with his practicality in particular is very effective as a "role model".

What of Rome itself, in this period? To the contemporaries in the mid-late fifties the general outlook was optimistic. The great days of Augustus (died A.D. 14) were remembered and, after Tiberius, the mad Gaius Caligula and even dear old Uncle Claudius, the young Nero aged seventeen at his accession, seemed like a breath of fresh air. New ideas were abroad when Nero arrived at power in October 54, roughly contemporary with the Christian interest of the Jerusalem conference on circumcision when, in effect, their door to freedom was kicked wide open. The first few years of the reign (54-68) were characterized by a struggle of family in-fighting; the emperor's tutor Lucius Annaeus Seneca supported him, but Britannicus son of the late Claudius was poisoned in 55. Seneca (c. 4B.C. – A.D. 65) closely contemporary with Paul, was a Stoic essayist and poet who became the young Nero's officiate in 49, holding consular rank and functioning as Prime Minister in the first five years of Nero. However, amid the court environment of men and women poisoning each other he retired from public affairs in 62 and with the poet Lucan, was killed in 65. Seneca's brother Novatus, subsequently called Gallio was the procurator in Achaia (Corinth)with whom Paul had dealings in 51-52; did the Apostle befriend the Roman here? An exchange of Seneca correspondence with Paul is known of and has generally been considered spurious, but this status is by no means certain. The reference at Philippians 4:22 of greeting from those of the Roman court may be literal, and there seems to be nothing in Seneca's writing hostile to what Paul represented. He believed in a principle that suffering provides an advantage of

LUCIUS ANNAEUS SENECA
From A First-Century Marble Bust

spiritual discipline further giving opportunity to exercise virtue. The ancient Roman legalistic religion was prevented, in the previous five or six centuries, from developing as a code of morals accommodated into worship, by the influx of foreign pagan influences, from which in reaction a suppression and holding in check of Orientalist cults has become a main home interest of Romans in regard to their own religious development, if any, and they saw Christianity only as another such foreign cult.

In this general environment a Christian outreach actually in Rome would have little chance of success, especially after Nero began to wobble in 62. Indeed, any real and rapid progress of this faith system would be likely to find an increasing hostile hatred in rival interests. With little interest in politics Nero amused himself with singing and horse-racing, leaving affairs largely in the hands of Seneca in the years 54 to 62. When he repudiated his wife Octavia and had her executed 9 June 62 her numerous supporters plotted against him and if they, as Nero's new enemies were behind professional arsonists as is believed, the Christian community was set fair to be caught in the "crossfire" when a fire was set in 64 near to the imperial palace in a project to infuriate the public against Nero by attributing the substantial fire damage to him, but from which he would then be desperate to recover some public regard.

While Paul was working here he enjoyed the company of at least nine other salient brethren from elsewhere largely, who are named in Colossians 4: 7-14. It seems certain that in 60-62 when they felt a confident optimism Paul of Ephesus and Epaphras of Colossae decided to write to each others' churches. The Epistles here were written together, Ephesians within a few days, at most, of Colossians. Paul's exquisite little letter to Philemon of either Colossae or nearby Laodicea seems to have been written at this time, a letter disclosing a great deal of diplomatic tact and skill developed in Paul's recent few years down to 61. Colossians and Ephesians are both letters of a general kind, with intention to strengthen the communities in their faith: against heresy at

Colossae and against falsehood and evil influences at Ephesus. By similarities beyond coincidence the Pastoral Epistle First Timothy indicates that Barnabas was acquainted with the Ephesians letter – he may have been also in Rome in about 62 when Titus was written, and the recollection about one named Onesiphorus (of Ephesus) coming to his aid there (2 Timothy 1:16-17) is noted, "he was not ashamed of my chain". Colossians and Philemon Mark the acme of Paul's Christian career and, together with Ephesians, showed a somewhat luxurious environment at least for the moment in which by their capacity to work together they could aspire to bear fruit outward to distant communities not yet met by the writer of a high letter thence. Such writings also bear witness to their freedom in a secular sense, notwithstanding occasional references to confinement as in Colossians 4:3 and 4:18, Ephesians 6:20 although possibly the meaning is of being in the bonds of the gospel, the believer taking Christ's yoke upon himself.

At a late time and possibly in 63 when Paul wrote to the Philippians he sensed a prospect of personal martyrdom, especially visible in the text at Phil. 2:16-17 of life ending: "... that I may rejoice in the day of Christ, that I have not run in vain nor laboured in vain; yea, and if I be offered upon the sacrifice and service of our faith, I rejoice with you all". A sudden eruption of tirade against judaizing in Philippians 3: 2-6 recalls the old Galatian problem, where either Paul had received news of such thing now in the Philippian community, or he was finding it active among the oppositions fast developing in his own location at Rome; but the former seems more likely. Other letters between Paul and the Philippians existed, from Phil 3:18 "Many walk, of whom I have told you often", when the Apostle is not known to have visited this community after first traveling onward therefrom. There is little doubt that the surviving Epistle was a reply letter to a communication from Philippi, vide Phil. 1:12, 1:4-5 and 2:19-30 giving reassurance and remembrance. If Luke went home from Rome to Macedonia it would stimulate one of the

Macedonian churches to write, evoking the same warmth in the reply as is seen in Paul's earlier letter to Thessalonica written in somewhat parallel circumstances; as Luke mentions two years in his knowledge of Paul in Rome, this suggests early 62 as a date for his own departure from the city, about a year before Philippians was written and some two years before Luke settled down to the task of writing the original Acts of Apostles.

It seems likely that Luke accumulated material for intended books at Jerusalem in mid-57 to autumn of 59 when other activities were at a standstill upon the procurators holding Paul. Then James would be his major source for the first half of Acts; the text in Acts 21:18 says that on arrival at Jerusalem Paul's retinue met James "and all the elders were present" – the absence of other apostolic names here suggests Simon Peter and John had left the city at some time between 54 and 57. Some material, and especially Sayings later added to Mark such as the verbal components of Sermon appearing in Luke 6:20-49 and 12:22-34 the Twelve disciples had heard the sayings. In this connection it is worth noting that Luke 6:20 combined with Mark 3:13 gives the occasion of Christ's Sermon on the Mount (not recorded by Mark) as that when, taking aside the ordained Twelve into a private place of "mountain" "He lifted up His eyes on His disciples" and gave them now the Sermon as an important inaugural address: where the St. Matthew author at 5:1 says "And seeing the multitudes, He went up into a mountain; and when He was set, His disciples came unto Him", the prospect is that the general mob was left behind, but this is not visible at Luke 6:19-20. Very likely we owe a great deal to James for the preservation of gospel materials apart from Simon Peter for Mark and of course independently St. John; James is also likely behind the St. Matthew author, in the Jewish Church. Luke's Preface to Acts points to a Proto-Luke as his former treatise unknown but possibly written up unpublished, from collected material, at Rome in 60 or 61. The Preface on Luke's later published gospel in the eighties shows a church requirement having developed against numerous attempts in such writing, that some need was seen by then to preserve accuracy and orthodoxy. This preface should be read as continuing straight into Luke 3:1 picking up his intended starting point for Luke, who always put his sources into his own words, and did not change his style. The abrupt switch between the heroic character of Jewish interest visible in Luke 1 and 2 contrasting with Luke's Attic Greek, coupled with the fact of the Christian-Jew split existing by the eighties, makes a later Lucan writing or even inclusion – of this Birth Narrative unlikely. No meeting of Luke with Simon Peter is known of, nor any connection of Luke with Antioch in Syria. Written in the early sixties before Luke had met Barnabas, the book of Acts of Apostles was not much used until after 180; it was not known to Marcion for instance at Rome in about 130, but by the end of the second century at least two forms of its text had emerged from copyings made after connections with living memory had been lost.

It was probably in the year 64 that Mark undertook to transmit direct knowledge of the holy ministry of Jesus by writing a gospel account which would include numerous details then considered to be necessary for such project. In this, he was taking up Simon Peter's doctrinal concern with the cross and the resurrection by applying an amplification with description of some history of the Lord's earthly career, simultaneously satisfying the desire of some luminaries that something should be done to put the future in remembrance, that indeed the knowledge should not be lost. No doubt Mark realized the immense importance of the project, for it is evident from the contents and style of writing in the work that he took it up in a thoroughly workman like manner, avoiding any tendency to gloss. His mother's house in Jerusalem was used by Jesus at the end of His ministry, and by Acts 12:12 for some ten years after that by the original brethren; and although the youth who followed the priests' rented mob to the Garden of Gethsemane and had his sleeping *dhoti* ripped from him (Mark 14:51) is not named, it can hardly be anyone else than Mark himself – they had gone firstly to that house and dawn blank before Iscariot further guided them to the garden where (John 18:2) the betrayer knew that Jesus was likely to be found. The disturbance had dragged the youth out of bed, and it would be natural for him to find an interest in learning details of what was behind it; if true, this was the starting-point for Mark's association, and he would surely get substantial familiarization of knowledge from discussions with those who had been with Jesus prior to this. The second-century father Papias testifies that Simon Peter was his principal source, but undoubtedly there were others in addition, and the whole matter of doing the gospel project is likely to have been taken in hand in association with Simon Peter near the time when Simon wrote his General Epistle. In the effort to produce this gospel the motivation for it reflects the extent of changes which had occurred between the thirties and the sixties, because people in the earlier period were full of their present-day euphoria with no evident immediate need to look beyond while they yet held a widespread expectation that Jesus would shortly return, an expectation which faded only gradually. As late as the mid-fifties Paul wrote in 1 Thessalonians 1:10 of their turning to God involved "waiting for His Son from heaven, whom he raised from the dead"; but when Luke wrote the Book of Acts not more than a decade later he was careful to include the definite statement at Acts 1:7, "It is not for you to know the times or the seasons which the Father hath put in His own power". Luke and Mark were younger men, and if Mark had been the youth (of say, sixteen or seventeen) in Gethsemane he would be aged about forty-eight when he wrote the gospel, Luke perhaps a few years younger and also in his forties at that time.

Taking the date of the Gospel according to St. Mark as 64, the writing was that of a Palestinian Jew thinking in Aramaic but writing in Greek of a coarse koine vernacular form with Semitic connectives pulled into Greek, though additionally at Mark 7:25-29 there is a play on words in the Greek with gunhi (a woman) and kunhi (a dog) and some Latin words are borrowed such as

Praetorium, centurio, quadrans; but Mark preferred Aramaic terms where other vocabulary might not be inevitable: Dalmanutha (for the town of Magdala), B'ney Regesh (3:17), Talitha cumi (5:41), Corban (7:11), Ephphatha (7:34), Abba (14:36), Golgotha (15:22) and Eloi, Eloi, lama sabachtani (15:34). This is writing with a considerable cosmopolitan character. Undoubtedly the authority for a gospel project at the time was vested in connecting back to the original disciples in an environment where wide still-living memories would not allow any fiction to pass. This writing down of the gospel history knowledge was part of a bloom of early religious awareness to practically serve a propagation and growth of the faith system beyond the deaths of those yet holding its torch. If done in 64 clearly Mark, who had been in Rome (Colossians 4:10), was no longer there but perhaps back in Antioch. Or, expressed in another way, the Gospel of Mark would be written just the same if the Christian outreach in Rome had succeeded. Certainly the St. Mark gospel project is visibly the foundation for the later projects of Luke and Matthew, written for somewhat different purposes; yet strangely as it seems, the contemporaries apparently had little idea as to what to do with this literary jewel of multicultural ethos.

From the point of view of Christendom as a whole, significant things were happening in the sixties. It was a time of new changes resulting in matters generally not being as they had been, in a sense that the early period with its straightforward simplicity was now lost. The surviving Apostles knew that in the natural order of things they had not a great deal of time remaining to them, things were moving on, and there was no clear certainty regarding the future. James was murdered in 62, and it seems certain that Paul was killed when the Christian community in Rome was wiped out in 64 – at least, it is difficult to see how he could escape the purge of Nero when the Christians there were collected as scapegoats ostensibly because of the city fire but also, according to Tacitus, "to glut one man's (i.e. Nero's) cruelty". There is a general agreement that the Pastoral Epistles were all three written by the same author, which is here taken further in a belief that the author was St. Barnabas who, by Titus 1:5 was at some time working in the upromising mission field of Crete and left Titus in charge of a Christian outreach there. A reasonable estimate of dates in these Epistles is in 62, Second Timothy in 65, and First Timothy in 67; and the three letters show something of the contemporary environment as being loaded with recent difficulties.

The Epistle to Titus was written by a man not very happy with the use of the pen, against a backdrop of unsuccess in the island of Crete. His estimate of the men of the country was not high; "One of themselves, a prophet of their own, said, The Cretans are always liars, evil beasts, show bellies. This witness is true". The original coiner of this adage could not be a Cretan, for that would destroy the logic in it: if he was a Cretan he was lying, and such witness must be untrue. However, this ancient adage appears to have originated in mainland Greece with one Epimenides, a Greek poet. In the address to Titus "My true child in a common faith" would come more strongly from Barnabas as the advocate from their early days at Antioch, probably before Paul was brought there. On the one hand Titus appears to have been regarded by Paul as a Christian leader in whom he had every confidence, as evidenced in Second Corinthians yet on the other he is, in the letter to Titus, apparently a man needing substantial guidance – a different view from Barnabas, but very likely a difference is accounted in the difficulties they were up against in Crete, where the outreach certainly seems to have been dying. Certainly Barnabas had confidence in him if he left Titus in charge of the work amid those difficulties, and the flow of the letter gives direction specifically applicable to the local oppositions. Heresies began to emerge at an early date, for Paul was aware of such deviance when he wrote from Rome at the beginning of the sixties at Colossians 2:8: "Beware lest any man spoil you through philosophy and vain deceit... after the rudiments of the world, and not after Christ". Now at Titus 3:10 Barnabas advises: "A man that is an heretic, after the first and second admonition reject, leaving him in self-condemnation". In Crete they were opposed by an agglomeration of judaizers and "many unruly and vain talkers and deceivers, specially they of the circumcision", among whom were various pagans. This country was a poor prospect for early Christian outreach, a material with which probably none could really work – in reality they were attempting the impossible and Titus had been left with a hopeless task in this land. Indeed, the text in 2 Timothy 4:10 suggests that the mission to Crete failed altogether at some time between 62 and 65: "Demas hath forsaken me, having loved this present world and is departed unto Thessalonika, Crescens to Galatia, Titus unto Dalmatia". Seemingly these men had been working as a team in Crete but then gave up altogether, going their separate ways which perhaps entailed their going home. Nothing is known of Crescens, but Titus had earlier been associated with Paul in West Greece and Demas likewise in Rome (Philippians 4:10); the note of them now to Timothy gives a strong impression that they went back to the secular. Titus probably was a Roman since, besides the name the country of Dalmatia in those days would interest only Romans, and it may well have been his home. Nothing more is heard of Christian work in first century Crete.

In an overall way the Pastoral Epistles show that institutional Church order and the establishment of a firm foundation of faith rooted in apostolic tradition had been developing outside of Paul in the fifties. The only visible candidate for a geographical centre in this is Antioch in Syria but, wherever the location, the formulation of church order originated in the ethics of family life; and as the Church grew partly as a bulwark against heresy, it was seen as an extended family involving confessions and credal unity. Much of this emerges with the circular letter named for Ephesians and written perhaps by Epaphras within Paul's knowledge or possibly under his direction in about 60, but it is taken onward in the Epistles to Titus and Timothy, three letters well named collectively as pastoral. Barnabas' use and understanding of the term bishop is early, first appearing at Titus 1:7, and the Episcopal office may have originated at Antioch. There is a vigorous pressure to the conclusion that after the mid or late fifties Christians in that city, perhaps including Simon Peter, Barnabas and Mark working there together felt an increasing need to organize the growing communities as an independent sanctuary against, and separate from, the outside world: that the earlier individual freedom to come and go simply among each others' houses, was no longer sufficient to guarantee the carrying forward of the Christian torch. Was Paul ever aware of this? Probably not, because his separate endeavour, long captivity in Jerusalem and Caesarea and this removal to the then Christian backwater of Rome meant isolation from the happenings beyond his own circuit of activity. In fine, the splendid first bloom of the Christian faith following was lopped off in order to necessarily strengthen the plant – in the mechanism intended to truly represent the holy gospel faith and knowledge in human lives St. John's "Abide in Him" (1 John 2:28) was eventually replaced with Ignatius' "Obey your Bishop" (Ign. Eph. 2) As both these references were written near the turn of the first to second century, on either side of it, this is a valid comparison. That early bloom has not grown again even yet, since it must be rooted in the independently individual hearts and minds of believers beyond mere dependence upon obedience to professional office-bearers; the familiar model of the flock under a shepherd is useful and good, but it does not take the high matter of believing faith all the way.

To recapitulate, by the time Barnabas came to write the Epistle second Timothy in about 65 the general Christian position did not look bright. Paul and James were dead, and whatever missionary outreach had been tried in Crete had apparently crashed in the years 62 to 65. Men who had been close and trusted co-workers with Barnabas had forsaken him. The event which must have involved Paul in Rome finally is described briefly by the Roman historian Tacitus in his "Annales" thus: "But all human efforts, all the lavish gifts of the emperor, and the propitiations of the gods, did not banish the sinister belief that the conflagration" (several city blocks destroyed in Rome in 64) "Was the result of an order. Consequently, to get rid of the report, Nero fastened the guilt and inflicted the most exquisite tortures on a class hated for their abominations, called Christians by the populace. Christus, from whom the name had its origin, suffered the extreme penalty during the reign of Tiberius at the hands of one of our procurators, Pontio Pilatus, and a most mischievous superstition thus checked for the moment, again broke out not only in Judaea, the first source of the evil, but even in Rome, where all things hideous and shameful from every part of the world find their centre and become popular. Accordingly, an arrest was first made of all who pleaded guilty; then, upon their information, an immense multitude was convicted, not so much of the crime of firing the city, as of hatred against mankind. Mockery of every sort was added to their deaths. Covered with the skins of beasts, they were torn by animals and perished, or were nailed to crosses, or were doomed to the flames and burnt to serve as a nightly illumination when daylight had expired. Nero offered his gardens for the spectacle, and was exhibiting a show in the circus, while he mingled with the people in the dress of a charioteer or stood aloft in a car. Hence, for criminals who deserve extreme, and exemplary punishment, there arose a feeling of compassion; for it was not, as it seemed, for the public good, but to glut one man's cruelty, that they were being destroyed. "Tacitus' "immense multitude" was an exaggeration, unless others besides the Christians were dragged in, because the Christian population in forties-to-sixties Rome was certainly not large. From this report it is certain that the community was wiped out; and for at least the rest of the century it is virtually certain that the Christians had no community as such, in Rome, although there are indications of a very few believing individuals of higher rank there late in the first century. As he possessed Roman citizenship Paul was likely to have been beheaded, rather than thrown to the public "entertainment" like a common cultic Jew.

On the positive side Barnabas and perhaps Simon Peter still lived, as did St. John who, however, was not known of across the middle of the century. Mark was busy on his gospel project and Luke, who seems to have been in Jerusalem presumably with James in 58 and 59 while Paul was in Roman hands, wrote his history "Acts (or, in the Greek "deeds") of Apostles" slightly later in about 63. In our general belief that Luke collected traditional transmitted gospel knowledge material over a number of years, he would certainly have been able to do this if he had association with James during a long lull in the wider activities. The note in 2 Timothy 4:11 shows that by 65 he had met Barnabas, and the marked paucity of data about this Apostle in the Book of Acts points to a strong probability that Acts was written before this meeting. Here Barnabas says also, "Take Mark, and bring him with thee" (i.e. Timothy) "for he is profitable to me for the ministry"; and then, "Bring the books, especially the parchments". This could refer to St. Mark's newly written gospel account, but in any event as three fair weather men had left him to go their separate ways, it is understandable that Barnabas should feel a need to have the company of his young protégé Timothy and his nephew Mark. The mention of the place Troas here at 2 Timothy 4:13 would involve a journey between East and West Greece, and verse 20 ibid appears to indicate Barnabas having made a journey to Corinth from Ephesus via Miletus. By the previous verse, if Aquila and Priscilla (2 Timothy 4:19) were back at Ephesus they obviously had escaped the Nero purge at Rome by a lucky chance of no longer being there. Coupling with the name of Onesiphorus where Timothy is asked to remember the writer, plus the verse at 2 Timothy 1:16-18, Ephesus was where Timothy received this letter, Barnabas having recently traveled away from there. That part of text shows Barnabas to have been in Rome at some time earlier, but it was possibly in the early sixties when he wrote to Titus. In the names with the writer at 2 Timothy 4:21 Erastus was the city treasurer at Corinth, but the Roman names Eubulus, Pudens, Linus and Claudia are hopelessly unknown, for all these names were common Latin praenoma.

From the letters to Timothy clearly this was a young man; the expressions "Let no man despise thy youth" (1 Timothy 4:12) and "Flee also youthful lusts" (2 Timothy 2:22) construe for a youth which normally means an age range of seventeen to twenty-two, which would estimate his birth year somewhere in the mid-forties. The writer's knowledge of his protégé's family indicated in 2 Timothy 1:5 and 3:15 suggests that he knew the family back in Cyprus and presumably in the later forties when he returned there with Mark after splitting up with Paul. In the earlier letter his intention was to encourage Timothy in a way which suggests that the young co-worker was newly engaged in participation with the work at Ephesus. From 2 Timothy 1: 16-17 Barnabas had been under duress at Rome, and there is an appearance of his being there when the letter to Titus was sent because, at Titus 3:13 one named Tychicus is named to relieve Titus for a visit in the writer's intention to spend the winter at Nicopolis, a place not mentioned elsewhere, and Tychicus (Ephesians 6:21) was also named as an emissary in the Ephesians Epistle written at Rome in about 61. By this, Tychicus seems to have been at the disposal of those working there with Paul at the time, including Barnabas; but from Titus 3:13 Apollos was then in Crete. In the later letter first Timothy Barnabas more fully developed the guiding advice which he had given to Titus, pertaining to elder and younger men and women, also servants, but now with amplification of detail and an addition of elders and deacons in the Church, particularly onward to requirements for the Episcopal office where the components in the list of them strongly point to a probability that the bishop's office was new, because when some time established there could be no need to spell out what will be necessary in a candidate – the qualifying points would soon become a matter of course. Altogether the professional tone of First Timothy shows a change in that the young man was now seen, some two years after the earlier letter, as an "ocean going" churchman to be depended upon with the future reckoned to be safe in his hands: there is a considerable contrast from the earlier atmosphere of the youthful novice needing personal encouragement with inclusion of reference back to his childhood.

It seems certain that direct movement towards manifestation of the believing brethren as an institutional body operating with organized administration sharply increased in the sixties between the time of writing of the Ephesians Epistle and that of First Timothy: that is, in the first half of this decade. Ephesians 2:19-22 plus 3:14-21 and 4:25 definitely saw the Church as existing in the hearts of individual believers united as fellow citizens of the household of God and thereby analogous to a building with Christ as the foundation cornerstone. But in 1 Timothy 5:16 Barnabas says, "Let not the Church be charged", indicating a collected form of centrally governed body which would, with his mention and some elaboration of the bishop, have a developed administrative form functioning on the Episcopal office. In 1 Timothy 1:3 where Barnabas says he left Timothy at Ephesus while himself traveling in Macedonia there is indication of an authority figure of a kind which neither Paul, Simon Peter in the Peter Epistle, nor the writer of Ephesians ever point: "That thou might charge some that they teach no other doctrine"; and the setting out of requirements for church office-bearers (1 Timothy 3:1-13) can only imply that Timothy, to whom "I write unto thee, hoping to come unto thee shortly", had authority to apply such standards beyond his own demeanor. Not long before, Timothy had simply been enjoined to preach in an activity of giving his own sermons (2 Timothy 4: 1-5) amounting just to a change on him to do the work of an evangelist as, no doubt, Titus had been doing in Crete. Beyond that, the earlier letter outside of its personal parts is confined to confirming confidence of Timothy in the faith. With 1 Timothy 4:14 there is a hint of ecclesiastical procedure apparently done at Ephesus within the two years period between the Timothy letters: "Neglect not the gift that is in thee by prophecy, with the laying on of the hands of the presbytery": it seems that so far there had been no bishop to do it.

It is reasonable to suppose that Barnabas was acquainted with the Epistle to the Ephesians when he wrote the Pastoral

Epistles, because certain similarities of the topics handled take the comparison beyond coincidence. Notably this includes the analogy of soldiering, on which the Ephesians author had taken a model in Ephesians 6:11-17, the Christian soldier in armour to oppose the invisible influences of evil beyond the flesh: it is picked up in 2 Timothy 2:1-4 where the young and inexperienced Timothy is visualized as just such a soldier, potentially as yet. Earlier to Titus we have the observations: "We were in the lusts of the flesh in the past, but God's love cured it" (Ephesians 2: 3-4 and Titus 3: 3-4); "By grace we are saved, not according to what we have done" (Ephesians 2: 8-9 and Titus 3:5); "Put away all bitterness and evil speaking" (Ephesians 4:31-32 and Titus 3:2 extending into the foregoing). Barnabas was similarly relaying something of Ephesians to Timothy: "We are called to salvation in knowledge of His will, according to His own purpose (Ephesians 1:9 and 2 Timothy 1:9); "He hath chosen us in Christ before the foundation of the world' (Ephesians 1:4 and 2 Timothy 1:9); Christ's descent and ascension (Ephesians 4:9-10 and 1 Timothy 3:16). The advising to be applied to wives appears in 1 Timothy 6:5-8; and whereas the Ephesians author included children, fathers and masters in Ephesians 6, Barnabas took these advising forward into the realm of church office-bearers. Hence the Pastoral Epistles to some extent overlap with Ephesians, but the latter was a general Church Epistle with little sign of the organizational aspect in the former.

Undoubtedly Barnabas and Simon Peter, themselves now aged in their early seventies which certainly in those days would be regarded as old men, saw the men of the younger generation such as Mark and Luke in their forties and Timothy just in his twenties, as the safe hands for the future shortly to come. In the latter days of these two Apostles who may have died in the late sixties only two strongly prominent centers of Christianity were flourishing: Antioch and Ephesus. By the time they died some centers, and certainly Antioch, had become less Presbyterian and perhaps less democratic than had everywhere been the normal state among the earlier communities of egalitarian assembled worshippers so familiar to Paul, communities of a kind to whom Paul, Simon Peter and the Ephesians author had addressed their Epistles with the idea of public readings. The first step on a thousand miles journey had been taken towards the system of authority from the top down, eventually to become a vast hierarchical and even monarchic system enthroning its bishops. There is no show without Punch; but it was to lead to extraordinary schismatic results unforeseeable at the time, all these things never seen nor needed in Hindu or Islam. The Church would survive, but it would not be a building fifty framed together as Ephesians 2:21 expresses it, nor Simon Peter's royal priesthood of a peculiar people (1 Peter 2:9) for many centuries. The first-century luminaries could not be expected to realize all the dangers inherent in their early steps, that while certainly it was imperative to strengthen Christendom by all available and acceptable means against drift, heresy and persecution, there might be similar need to guard against the tares in every individual within the profession of Christianity as well as outside it: and the tares and the wheat cannot be separated in this world's life. Back in 2 Corinthians 2:10-11 Paul had warned about uncharitability in lack of a forgiving nature being apt to push aside a necessary forbearance, in terms of Satanic influence gaining its advantage when we are not ignorant of Satan's devices. The sixties was a rough period separating the balmy earliest days from the never-certain later times, and in some ways Christendom did not come out of that decade unscathed.

8
The Seventies

Besides a drifting of Christianity into, or towards, an organizational world, two further negative things characterized the seventies. There had been Judaic opposition to the new faith of the Nazarins from the beginning, but as the century went on a seriously deep and widespread rift between the faiths was developing, and its effects were first felt in this decade; in addition a tendency to heretical deviations was growing apace. In some ways these things were interconnected not only in arising or becoming more marked at the one time but in character, and also they shared in the failure of believing brethren to either ameliorate or remove them. In the earlier time of St. Paul the term heresy meant merely a sect or faction which was understood as a philosophical school holding some particular doctrine, in Hellenistic Greece whose language he used and to whose people he brought salvation. To contemporary Jews, Christianity was itself heretical as being regarded as a sect of the Nazarins, and the judaizers opposing Paul along his travel routes clearly saw him as a heretic in the same sense which Christians would later take up that of heresy literally against orthodoxy. In 1 Corinthians 11:18-19 Paul was aware of some degree of division already in a community, but saw it as a necessary thing in a proving connection: in the mid-fifties they had as yet little idea of any breaking away as leading to ecclesiastical schism. By the early sixties Paul sought to warn brethren at Colossae, a church he never visited, against persons then regarded as heretics (Colossians 2:4, 2:6, 2:8): "And this I say, lest any man should beguile you with enticing words: as ye have received Christ Jesus the Lord, so walk ye in Him. Beware lest any man spoil you through philosophy and vain deceit, after the tradition of men, after the rudiments of the world, and not after Christ". It is possible that this was a reaction to news of at least one self-opinionated teacher having menaced the small community by making unacceptable inroads there, a possibility almost certainly characterizing the trickle of heresy at its beginning. The earliest form taken by heretics in the Christian field was a denial of the sufficiency of Christ Jesus to redeem from sin or to manifest the revelations of God; and in his appalling error they admixed a pagan input of astrological junk. In general comparisons it was a syncretistic cult on a pagan base drawing from Jewish sources by people who had not been convinced in the Christian truths and yet who desired some spiritual uplift and tried to satisfy this desire by building their own house in vain out of an a la carte selection. We know that heresies along these lines were seriously increasing across the seventies, but it is impossible to identify any heresiarchs in this decade or to show to what extent the errors penetrated particular churches. However, the fact that the church at Colossae is not mentioned among the churches of Asia in the Seven Letters (Rev. 2 and 3) suggests at least a possibility that by the late seventies when these letters of divine inspiration were written, heretical attacks had finished it off.

The earliest indication of collective effort to take up arms in the emerging struggle of orthodoxy against heresy is given by the Epistle of St. Jude which, allowing ten years or more to have elapsed in the slow development, may have been written in the mid-seventies. Like his presumably elder brother James Alphaeus (Mark 3:18 with Luke 6:16) Jude describes himself not as an Apostle as Simon Peter and Paul had done but as "the servant of Jesus Christ". Similarly also, he was writing for the Jewish Church, a church which was no longer in Jerusalem after the city had been destroyed in 70 and one whose leader had been changed when James died back in 62. According to Hegesippus James' successor was another relative named Symeon; but the Jewish Church had already faded into insignificance, being not aided by the currently growing Christian-Jew split, and in this diminution Jude was extending his view outwards to "the common salvation" of verse 2. In verse 4 he confirms that heretics had penetrated into church communities as separatists who would not submit to apostolic authority. Jude's Epistle appears bleak in its topic of third-rate people who have fallen away into errors: "ungodly men", "filthy dreamers", "complainers walking after their own lusts". But in his final few verses 20-25 we find a confirmation of his nickname Lebbeus Thaddeus (Matthew 10:3 from Mark 3:18) which means Jude "the all-heart", as he enjoins the spirit of the sermon on the Mount in forwarding a method for dealing with these idiots whose errors might, for all the believer knows, be arisen through no fault of their own: "And of some have compassion, making a difference; and others save with fear, pulling them out of the fire" – as lepers cleansed of their formerly spotted flesh. In verse 24 there is no mistaking the strong implication that, but for the grace of God, any one of us might have been similarly amongst those lowest of the low; nobody else reached such high level of forbearance as this, not even St. John. The Epistle of Jude could possibly have been stimulated by the failure of one or more churches in Asia Minor, such as Colossae, and in the same possibility there is no appeal in it to established clergy – St. Jude was still speaking to the undifferenced assembly of all brethren in the same manner as those Epistles earlier than the Pastorals. Although later than Barnabas by some eight or ten years, Jude gives no impression of Clergy and laity distinction, but his letter does indicate an existing unity of ordered life in the community called Church which heretics were undermining and undercutting as "hidden rocks" intruding into the love feasts of the faithful (Jude 12).

Of St. John's whereabouts between Jerusalem in the forties and Patmos island much later, we have no direct record. Before the forties he had worked in Samaria where, at the town of Gitta (the home town of Justin Martyr who testifies) he and Simon Peter had collided with a romancer named Simon Magus as described in the eighth of Acts. After Patmos he wrote the fabulous Fourth Gospel wherein his obvious affection for Samaria, visible in John 4, suggests a possibility that he spent a long stretch of years in this land of central Palestine. Such a thing would mean a departure from his roots of Judaic culture, and this seems to appear in his habitual form of lumping together all oppositions to Jesus in his gospel narrative as "the Jews", which would be a Samaritan habit as much as anything else. The likelihood is that, after leaving Jerusalem in about 43 he did not return to Judaic surroundings throughout the rest of his long life. The fact that John finds no mention in connection with any of the Christian centers across the middle decades of the first century, and this for such one of the principal Apostles, points to a practical certainty that he was working in locations which lay outside all of their known endeavours of outreach. This in the contemporary Christian geography would mean either Samaria or Egypt and for a few reasons the latter is less likely.

Across the middle of the first century Samaria was not a land of settled peace like Egypt, even under the pax Romana. Like the Jews the Samaritans, with mutual detestation between them, held the Hebrew Scriptures but they accepted only the five Moses books of the Torah comprising Genesis, Exodus, Leviticus, Numbers and Deuteronomy. Rome ruled both nationalities and was sometimes actively involved in peacekeeping fronts as when in about the year 48 some Galilean Jews were slain at Ginea village near the Samaria Galilee border. This resulted in a Jewish reprisal under a bandit Eleazar Ben Dineus in which a number of Samaritan villages were plundered in the usual way of these dacoits, so that the Roman procurator Cumanus took four regiments of foot against the Jewish interests, and also armed the Samaritans, an action which seems to have involved pacifying all of Samaria. If John was working then in the country he must have seen some of it. Quadratus the President of Syria came to Samaria, ordered the crucifixion of captives taken by Cumanus, and sent the Jewish ringleaders to Rome where Claudius had them executed. This state of ferment in Samaria was finally sealed when the dacoit Eleazar ben Dineus was caught by the next procurator Felix, who features with Paul in the late fifties, and sent to Rome. John is known to have been exiled, and if from Samaria it is likely to have been at a later date than 59 when Felix was replaced by Festus; the serving of an exilium was more probable when in about 73 the emperor Vespasian established new pagan communities as a deliberate policy at Nablus in Samaria, a country normally free of both pagans and Jews. There is little doubt that a forming of Christian communities in Samaria, with ite anti-Jew "purity" and its lack of proselytes capable of receiving the Christian outreach easily, would scarcely be possible. If John was there, he would perforce be obliged to operate at individual level, following the itinerant ministry methods of the Lord Jesus to individuals often aside from assembled crowds, which would not be out of character or peculiar to him.

VESPASIAN
Drawn From A Statue

In the commission of the disciples to travel out to other lands Luke notes in Acts 1:8 that their witnessing was to be carried specifically to Samaria and then further to "the uttermost part of the earth". To some extent they would all be aware of some practical difficulties in this, and it would be characteristic in either John or Thomas to attempt Samaria as a more difficult district. Although no church was known to be established here in the first century or indeed later, the Logos theology given peculiarly by St. John was not unknown among Samaritans. Writing his "Dialogue with Tyrpho the Jew" in about 135 Justin Martyr developed the doctrine of the Logos integral with the God of the Old Testament after associating with an aged Christian at home in Samaria who had put him through a test on Socratic lines. Justin says his soul was "bursting to hear the peculiar and choice secret of philosophy", and this seems to be a Samaritan version of the wider Greek dissatisfaction with pagan religious ideas which had given Paul a more, fruitful working material when he travelled among them. The main difference in Samaria was that, because of its Jewish roots, Christianity would be largely rejected in the population there, but might be confined to intellectuals separately though not in groups – something similar to Nicodemus coming at night for an interview with Jesus, as described by John in his gospel third chapter, as a man desiring to make his own enquiries. John could well be dealing in a more specialized way with philosophers; such experience can account for the factor of his gospel and the General Epistle First John being full to the brim with fellowship deriving from the contrast: at the personal level his glad response in the opening up afforded by the Gentile association at Ephesus late in his life is certainly visible. At Ephesus he enjoyed the society of good company and was appreciative of it as an environment not open to him since leaving Jerusalem in the forties, wherever he then went. His revulsion from "the Jews" of his own expression is clearly evident in John 7:13, "No man spake openly of him for fear of the Jews", which at this degree is not explained in terms only of Gentile contact first enjoyed in his old age.

In Revelation 1:9 John, unusually giving his name, says that he was confined on the Isle of Patmos, but the dates of his time there and his release are not known. It is quite possible that the sentence of exile was served under the emperor Vespasian, who knew the Aegean area intimately from his days of army service. In the Roman system self-banishment by which a person might avoid legal proceedings on conviction was available to persons who had Roman citizenship. This privilege is not known for the Zebedee family but John, like Paul may have possessed it as Jews often did. There is an unreliable tradition that on Patmos John worked in mines, which could be based from a grain of truth since it was under Vespasian that a lex data regulating the industry of mining was drawn up, in which banishment with a metalla mining connection was included. Also under Roman law an exilium was cancelled on the death of the emperor under whom it had been served which in St. John's case if under Vespasian would date in 79. On the hypothesis that he had beeen banished on difficulties arising from Vespasian's action regarding pagans in Samaria in 73 this suggests a six years spell on Patmos, a tiny island of only some thirty-four square kilometers extent.

By the late seventies probably all the other Apostles had departed this life, and there is no sign in the records that they had been in contact with John for many years, or that John had ever been in Asia Minor before his time on Patmos. This means that he did not know the churches of Asia to which he wrote the seven letters comprising Revelation 2 and 3; but these letters written by St. John's hand disclose an apostolic authority in which direct divine inspiration is certain: the authorship here is of the Lord Jesus. At about eighty kilometers Ephesus is not far distant from Patmos, and it is possible that churchmen on the Asia Minor mainland knew of John's location in exile by the late seventies and that by this or other related knowledge the Apostle's moving to Ephesus, which would become possible after the death of Vespasian, must surely have been effected. The fact that John uses the past tense in Revelation 1:9-11 of the point in time when he was commissioned to write to the specific churches and then send the letters to them confirms that the writing was done on the island, not afterwards. Because of his long period of years spent in isolation and out of touch with the Christian circuits, it is unlikely that John at the time of writing knew of the extent of the Christian outreach and of the existing communities in the area, notwithstanding their near proximity; he was long and deeply isolated until by some means contact was made in which a meeting by one or more of the Ephesus brethren seeking for John is very much more likely than the reverse. Looking back to much earlier times it is evident, from the Book of Acts, that he knew that accommodation with Gentiles had been achieved, because he was still at Jerusalem when Simon Peter made report of his work firstly involving them.

ON PATMOS ISLE
Revelation 1:9f.

Surely the unction of the Holy Spirit is continually at work in the world. In the period here considered some development of the Christian believers proceeding towards institutional organization had, from early signs in the Epistle to Ephesians, been progressing steadily in the decade between mid-sixties and mid-seventies. Was the coming rank-and-file structure needed to patch over failure, or to insure against it? If a few communities were no longer functioning by the later seventies, such as Crete, Colossae and perhaps Galatia, their demise would give cause for considerable concern. It could happen everywhere to communities small as yet, dwelling in a confused environment where, in the surrounding world some tried to reconcile Jewish beliefs with pagan notions while others attempted to interweave Christian teachings with units of Greek philosophy; in this regard it is even possible to detect some elements of Stoicism in St. Paul earlier. There are two grand points in connection with this contemporary environmental risk, perhaps visible in the timing of the Letters to the Seven Churches of Asia. Firstly St. John, the Apostle who in many ways had been closest to Jesus, was preserved in life by his isolation and now was indeed Christ's principal servant on earth. Just as none but God manifest in the man Jesus could accomplish the salvation by universal sacrifice in our stead, so similarly no other mortal man that John Zebedee could serve in the high manifestation of particular revelation given to the very young Christendom at a crossroads. Secondly in all piety as we believe the Letters to be wholly inspirational (as with the Classical Prophets by what the Hebrews called bath kol ("the daughter of the voice") there is no doubt of Christ's readiness to direct and bless the community of believers while they make proper use of the light of His word which shall not pass away, and His ordinances. In the Lord's providential government of the world, and of the Holy Spirit's work in it, mankind is not left abandoned with a freedom to wreck itself: this generation is in a necessary state of freewill, but there are limits. The letters are restricted to a chain of communities running from Smyrna southward to Laodicea, but no reason for this limitation can be known;

currently these may have been the only churches in the region, but Antioch, Thessalonika, Philippi and Corinth were also alive. Geographically the gift of the Letters applied only in East Greece, not in either Europe or the Roman province of Syria.

Literary analysis indicates that the Seven Letters were written in Greek and the Apocalypse in either Hebrew or Aramaic. If the former document was made in the koine or common Greek which was the language in widespread use in apostolic times it would be suitably familiar for the use of those to whom it was addressed, and certainly it contains nothing of the Hebraisms appearing in the latter. The Book of the Apocalypse was later translated by two or more hands, and John did not rework the book. They had difficulty in construing the Hebraic sense in a limited syntax, and some words such as hallelujah and amen would not go directly into Greek; there would be no general difficulty with vocabulary, since the Greek is a rich language with many more words for expression of meaning than the six thousand words limitation in Hebrew, where also the vowels have to be supplied. In rendering God of hosts from the Hebrew, phrases were sometimes split up when moved into the Greek to express the eternal power and Godhead with the identity of Jesus as in Revelation 1:7-8, and here the term Amen is qualified with an added emphasis on the Greek nai, "yes (indeed)". Perhaps the use of Hebrew in this era when the old dispensation had been superseded, which seems to make it redundant, was a factor to do with the seer St. John the Divine himself. His writing as commanded (Revelation 1:19) from the great sequence of visions over the hilly humps of Patmos (Greek bathmis ("steps") contains no sign of human intervention and, like the Classical prophets, it is unlikely that John wholly understood what was written; Isaiah, for instance, had no familiarity with anything current of the details about the Passion of Jesus which would be more than seven centuries future to his time. One difference in the Letters and the Apocalypse further is that whereas the Letters must involve direct inspiration in the writing, the Apocalypse was a straightforward report of things seen in the visions wonderfully vouchsafed to John in a physical way with the eyes. It seems certain that these two works of St. John on Patmos were written at different times, the Apocalypse later but not by much. John says that "after these things", that is, the writing of the Letters, he looked up and saw in vision an opening in the sky; not as given in the English Authorized Version "a door was opened" (with the "was" supplied in italics), which gives an impression of him seeing the action of it being opened, but Kai Idou Thura hin eowgmenhi en tow ouranow " a door set open (or, reined back) in the blue sky", as if it had already been thus but he had not observed it without a change in himself. The visions came through the theological quality and frame of the seer.

The text in Revelation 1: 10-20 testifies that John "in the Spirit on the Lord's Day" was rendered open to receive those things directly given to him with the command to write them in a book to be sent to the seven named churches, before beginning the work. Certainly the contents of the Letters leave no scope for assuming any other than divine power and authority beyond all possibility of any Christian luminary, even St. John, as the officiating origin. The vision of the Lord at the outset, as described with a serenity of composition where signs of mental agitation might naturally be expected, was one of brightness and power; but here St. John was acquainted with the Lord which must make the difference, a man already made exceptional, and he saw Jesus again now newly manifested in resplendent glory at the moment of commissioning him to receive and transmit an immense document for all church development at its historical beginning. In this the Seven churches of Asia along a six hundred kilometers chain from Pergamos in the north to Laodicea in the south may be fairly regarded as the Cradle of all Church: originally this is an Asian religion. Of the seven, only Ephesus is known of originally from Luke's Book of Acts and presumably the other six were founded in the late fifties to the early seventies. It is perhaps a useful exercise to collect the Letters into a single documentary unit standing above and beyond all human encyclicals, because in all subsequent ages we may continually find ourselves undeniably within the prescriptions here established at the beginning.

"I know thy works, and thy labour, and thy patience, and how thou canst not bear them which are evil: and thou hast tried them which say they are Apostles, and are not, and hast found them liars; and hast borne with patience, and for My name's sake hast labored, and not fainted. Nevertheless, I have against thee this: that thou hast left thy first love. Remember therefore, from whence thou are fallen, and repent, and do the first works; or else I will come unto thee quickly, and will remove thy candlestick out of his place, I thou repent. But this thou hast, that thou hatest the deeds of the Nicolaitans, which I also hate. To him that overcometh will I give to eat of the tree of life which is in the midst of the paradise of God.

I know thy works, and tribulation, and poverty (but thou art rich) and I know the blasphemy of them which say they are Jews and are not, but are of the synagogue of Satan. Fear none of those things which thou shalt suffer; behold, the devil shall cast certain of you into prison, that ye may be tried; and ye shall have tribulation ten days: be thou faithful unto death, and I will give thee a crown of life. He that overcometh shall not be hurt of the second death.

I know thy works, and where thou dwellest, even where Satan's seat is: and thou holdest fast My name, and hast not denied My faith, even in those days wherein Antipas was My faithful martyr, who was slain among those of Pergamos, where Satan dwelleth. But I have a few things against thee, because thou hast among you some that hold the doctrine or Balaam, who taught Balak to cast a stumbling block before the children of Israel, to eat things sacrificed unto idols, and to commit fornication. So hast thou also them that hold the doctrine of the Nicolaitans, which thing I hate. Repent; or else I will come unto thee quickly, and will fight against them with the sword of My mouth. To him that overcometh will I give to eat of the hidden manna, and will give him a white stone, and in the stone a new name written, which no man knoweth except he that receives it.

I know thy works, and charity, and service, and faith, and thy patience, and all thy works; and the last more than the first. Notwithstanding, I have a few things against thee, because thou dost suffer that women Jezebel, which calleth herself a prophetess, to teach and to seduce my servants to commit fornication, and to eat things sacrificed to idols. And I gave her space to repent of her fornication; and she repented not. Behold, I will cast her into a bed, but them that commit adultery with her into great tribulation, except they repent of their deeds. And I will kill her children with death; and all the Church shall know that I am He which searcheth the reins and hearts: and I will give unto the rest of those among you as many as have not this doctrine, and which have not known the depths of Satan, as they speak; I will put upon you none other burden than that which ye have already; hold fast till I come. And he that overcometh, and keepeth My works unto the end, to him will I give power over the nations: and he shall rule them with a rod of iron – as the vessels of the potter shall they be broken to shivers; even as I received of My Father. And I will give him the morning star.

I know thy works, that thou hast a name, that thou livest and art dead. Be watchful, and strengthen the things which remain, that they are ready to die: for I have not found thy works perfect before God. Remember therefore how thou hast received and heard, and hold fast, and repent. If therefore thou shalt not watch, I will come on thee as a thief, and thou shalt not know what hour I will come upon thee. Thou hast a few names even among you, which have not defiled their garments; and they shall walk with Me in white: for they are worthy. He that overcometh, the same shall be clothed in white raiment; and I will not blot out his name out of the Book of life, but I will confess his name before My Father, and before His angels.

I know thy works; behold, I have set before thee an open door, and no man can shut it; for thou hast a little strength, and hast kept My word, and hast not denied My name. behold, I will make them of the synagogue of Satan, which say they are Jews and are not, but do lie: behold, I will make them come and worship before thy feet, and to know that I have loved thee. Because thou has kept the word of My patience, I also will keep thee from the hour of temptation, which shall come upon all the world, to try them that dwell upon the earth. Behold, I come quickly: hold that fast which thou hast, that no man take thy crown. Him that overcometh will I make a pillar in the temple of My God, and he shall go no more out; and I will write upon him the name of My God, and the name of the city of My God, the new Jerusalem, which cometh down out of heaven from My God; and My new name.

I know thy works, that thou art neither cold nor hot; I would that thou wert cold, or hot. So then because thou are lukewarm, and neither cold nor hot, I will spur thee out of My mouth. Because thou sayest 'I am rich, and increased with goods, and have need of nothing'; and knowest not that thou art wretched, and miserable, and poor, and blind, and naked: I counsel thee to buy of Me gold tried in the fire, that thou mayest be rich; and white raiment, that thou mayest be clothed, and the shame of thy nakedness not then appear; and anoint thine eyes with eye-salve, that thou mayest see. As many as I love, I rebuke and chasten: be zealous therefore, and repent. Behold, I stand at the door and knock: if any man hear My voice, and open the door, I will come in to him and will sup with him, and he with Me. To him that overcometh will I grant to sit with My Father in His throne.

He that hath an ear to hear, let him hear what the Spirit saith unto the Church.

To the Church this is a foundation stone for all her future, an action of the Lord's doing, marvelous in our eyes. The seven packets here collated are of, respectively, Ephesus, Smyrna, Pergamos,

Thyatira, Sardis, Philadelphia, and Laodicea. With these churches originally addressed as being communities of believers, Ephesus as a city was smashed in A.D. 262 and Smyrna suffered martyrdom in A.D. 155; others may not have lived far into the future, but we do. This marvelous document of the Seven Letters marks a literary and theological point of watershed dividing the times before it, and after. The gospels of St. Luke and the St. Matthew author, although written in the eighties, really belong on this basis to the earlier time of St. Mark who, in re-issuing their projects largely from him was polished and amplified by them both. The books of the New testament canon written before 70, i.e. St. Mark, Acts of Apostles, St. Paul's Epistles, Ephesians, James, Peter, and the Pastoral Epistles are all splendidly worthy of inclusion in the canon of Orthodoxy, but there are degrees. In an important way they are at a lower level of holiness than the books written in the seventies and later, viz. Jude, Hebrews, and the writings of St. John. Generally across the smaller and later group of books Jude was writing to the Jewish Church of unknown location after the mid-sixties exhorting those brethren to "earnestly contend for the faith which was once delivered to the saints" (verse 3) as referring to the environment around the Apostles back in 33. The Book of Hebrews, a title inferred from the contents (but more suitably might be From the Hebrews) was not an Epistle but a homiletic apologia designed to explain the Messianic and intercessory offices of Jesus to all Christians in cultures where familiarity of such was not expected. In Hebrews however, there are no references to circumcision or to Jewish ritual law. Far more substantial than the letters of the brothers James and Jude, this author gave little attention to the matter of heretics and oppositions, but by contrast concentrated on the holding of true faith in the ordinary way: "But we are not of them who draw back unto perdition; but of them that believe to the saving of the soul" (Hebrews 10:39). This was a man who followed Jesus' injunction given at Mark 6:11, duly shaking from his feet the dust of unbelief and wasting no time on it. This is a wide comparison against Jude's whole concern that the brethren in the Jewish

Church might be swamped by a tide of "filthy dreamers"... crept in unawares". There is little likelihood of Jude and the Hebrews author writing in conscious knowledge of each others' project, though the two works were in all probability written nearby in time, in the first half of the seventies. The note at Hebrews 13:14 "Here we have no continuing city, but we seek one to come" applies in a time not long after their city, Jerusalem, had been destroyed by Roman army legions in 70. Possibly the Hebrews author had been in a location where not much was seen of the oppositions in the seventies while Jude on the other hand was definitely up against certain of the heretics; the style and use of types in this book points to Alexandria as the place of writng, with characteristics of style reminiscent of Philo (of Alexandria) who, however, habitually used allegories, and this may be another link possibly with Apollos (Acts 18:24). Hebrews does not show a knowledge of the references to oppositions contained in the letter to Pergamos as, for instance, the Nicolaitan sect, a name which as Nikowlatan means a person or people with an aim of stamping out genuine worship – evidently of evil inspiration. The name Antipas means "against all", a martyr at Pergamos which applies equally to St. Athanasius later, in the fourth century. One on God's side is a majority. Another meaning of a phrase which ought to be clarified is the refrence to being given a white stone. Throughout the Graeco-Roman Mediterranean stones were used for voting: white for the motion, black against.

The Book of Hebrews and the Johanine writings are works rising theologically with great directness; they are books to be read anywhere and digested into the Reader's individual life to him immense benefit. If the Church in the sixties had begun to gouge herself more deeply into the world, the Hebrews author and St. John do not appear as part of that but rather, if sincerely taken up, pull in a quite different direction. When you are in a hole, stop digging. It is regrettable that the identity of the Hebrews author is unknown, and we can only adhere to the guess of Apollos, without firm evidence elsewhere while no competitive candidate is in sight, certainly. Apollos was in Crete with Titus, according to Titus 3:13, and the Hebrews author knew Timothy as he says at Hebrews 13:23 "Know ye that our brother Timothy is set at liberty; and if he comes soon, I will bring him when I visit", which gives an appearance of this author belonging to whatever Christian circuit Timothy had joined. This author was a highly educated man writing in Greek with a syntax and vocabulary transcending the koine ordinary form and use of words generally used. If a comparison may be put in English dress to illustrate: whereas Mark might have written "And straightway the Pharisees came again to argue against Jesus"; with Luke, "The Pharisees were confrontational because they understood Him not"; but the author of Hebrews would use a more Oxbridgy expression, "The Pharisees opposed Him in so far as lively Philistines were not in vogue". His essentially three parts comprising the book, viz. Divine superiority of the son (Hebrews 1:1-4:13), Jesus' offices and sacrifice (4:14-10:18) and Exhortations (10:19-13:22) involve a sustained rhythm between ˋ handling and moral certainty. It is at the beginning of the Exhortation section that he stresses the universal individual appeal to the believer holding fast in true faith (10:19-25); in verse 24 here, "And let us consider one another to provoke unto Love and good works, not (to the extent of) forsaking the assembling of ourselves together, as some do"- in the first part of the verse *kai katanowmen allhilous eis paroxusmon agaphhis kai kalown ergon* the rendering might rather be "and understand one another for provoking affection and a call to a work". It is work in the singular, and the Greek does not say "good works" in the Jacobean and Church sense; and here "provoke" is meant in the sense of sharpening, like an edged tool for cleaner work since all the intensity of the term is meant, but not a transitoriness. This text rises above any merely philanthropic formula of considering others. To consider one another is a mark of the household of God.

The Hebrews author was not aware of St. John being still alive, and considered his present time to be now in a post-apostolic age, an era in which he offered such phrases as "these last days" (1:1) and "the world to come" (2:5) against a prospect or possibility that Christians might, in neglecting the disciplines of truth in faith, weaken through weariness, on which idea his method for remedy of the supposed prospect was to pull back to the Old Testament with its Hebrew foundation from which the Christians inherited. He was deeply conscious of dealing in new times, as is evident at the outset of his book where he establishes first of all the strong formula that God has spoken not through prophets as with His ancient servants, but through His directly representative own Son appearing personally and visibly in human nature as well as divine. This aspect of the Word made flesh (which we regularly regard as Johannine doctrine) was a fulfilling of everything, of which no principality of the earth could conceive. This whole matter of the appointment of the only-begotten Son of one substance with the Father had made known the glory and perfections of the Divine Creator. In the circumstances of the time when no New Testament canon of books yet existed the author of course used the Hebrew Scripture to make his reasoning points as Barnabas and Paul had done earlier, and as the author of the Epistle of Barnabas would be doing later. In effect the Christian System comes from the Hebrew culture, from their originally being monotheistically loyal (in principle though not in practice) to God. From the Hebrews author's method he reaffirms the greatness of the Saviour in His creation, the depths of the error from which He saves the worst of sinners who seek His salvation in their perishing need of it, and their freedom from cost against the price He paid to obtain it. If this immense gift of love beyond human understanding is rejected in the parallel gift of freewill, what have we got? And where is the escape?

Clearly by the Seventies the former expectation of an early return of the Lord Jesus in a Second Coming was no longer in anticipation. Similarly evident the Christian-Jews rift, as a general phenomenon, was now visibly widening. For the Hebrews author hope for the future is bound up in faith held in that future, under the promises of God: steadfastness and patience is demanded of the believer intrinsically with God's revelation in Christ Jesus, the Christian is to be a person of faithful profession and one whose life is modeled on Christ's example. In this provision Christ Jesus is our High Priest and Mediator at the mercy-seat of God, a priest upon His throne, the only means of effecting salvation unto reconciliation with God. This author does not explicitly refer back to the historic events of the Passion and Resurrection of Christ beyond just a note that God brought our Lord Jesus from the dead, in Hebrews 13:20; for Christian believers the essential knowledge of those events seems to be presupposed This author may have known of St. Mark's Gospel, as Timothy appears to have done (2 Timothy 4: 11-13). It is in this knowledge of the God-man made like as we are, to undergo the testing in the world and thereby to obtain successfully in the Christian faith the victory over death, that the believer is to rely on His capacity and power of mediation above all angelic mandate, in constant hope justified in that constant faith. Either the author saw a tendency of Christians falling away as the Jews had done along ancient times, through erroneous traditions of human invention jacked up with accepted authorities, or such thing actually emerging in times long future beyond him was remarkably coincidental. In Christianity we do not much believe in mere coincidence; to some degree this author, whoever he was, had the true prophetic gift.

After the depressing trough of the sixties and before the end of the seventies this man was in effect casting up a balance sheet of what adherence to Christianity meant, and ought to mean with others in future times. The Lord Jesus who triumphed over death by dying in innocent loneliness at the hands of sinning men, requires His followers to love as He loved, doing good works beyond what regular circumstances oblige them to do. What if earth be but the shadow of heaven and of things therein, with resemblance more than on earth is thought? The believers are hallmarked as such in making Him their practical guide, manifesting His Spirit in their own disposition and conduct, to be persons of example in whom He lives; they do not serve elsewhere to thus render to the Lord an unflinching disobedience.

It is perhaps interesting to us to follow a similar line and summarise the contemporary known picture of this royal faith before the beginning of the eighties. In Christ's revelation concerning mankind as a whole, it is clear that God's intention in the reconciling of humanity back to Himself – that which dwells in evoluted animal state but is not part of it – individuals are to become such as He was, in a projection of redeemed humanity transfigured towards a regenerated race inhabiting a renovated world. But this world is not set fair for such cleaning up; the blossom of betterment blooms here on the good tree, but the fruit is gathered elsewhere. Christ has shown us the Father and how He stands affected towards us, also ourselves and the prospect opened before us. In Him was both God and man, so that He was able to affirm the revelation not merely by spoken words but in particular by His life visible to us. He shows us the unbroken unity: in the Divinity is the nature of a Son to obey, to receive and to sacrifice, with a Father to command, to give and to bless with acceptance. In a divine ordination laid upon us the cross is ours as well as Christ's. One must have experienced hunger and thirst before one can rightly appreciate the true delight of gratifying the appetite; have known loneliness of heart before one can learn to crave for love; must fight through sickness to death's door, before the exquisite joy of returning health can be tasted. Sorrow must endure through the night, before joy cometh in the morning, winter be bleak, bare and bitter before we can revel in the warm beauties of spring. And if our life had no power to give pleasure, it would be incomplete as a year in which no roses bloom. If there were no cross, should any ever wear the crown?

In the natural temporal course secular successes, which ultimately leave higher cravings of the heart ungratified, can and do fail when health fails, love is wounded, or disabling age infirmity – to the stroke of death – descends upon our trust in the sensual. It is not required that a man be found gifted, powerful or influential in a life aiming only at prizewinning, pointless without success in it. Just finish the race, remembering that it is impossible to please God in dealing justly, loving mercy, and walking humbly with Him, without faith (Heb. 11:6). There is in the universe a power of God which loves right and which means to uphold the right against humankind's desire in opposite tendency for wrong. The cosmic battle between good and evil, which to us is a mystery, is not yours but God's; and if God's upholding ever failed in one point His Cause would be a failure, His universe lost. We are accountable to God, not to man, and therefore it behaves us to promote the common cause of truth and holiness: and we look forward, not back, with courage and a hope that will never make us ashamed, fully aware of our sinfulness but also knowing that the kingdom of heaven is within the believer who in selfless and steadfast obedience to God manifests his acceptance of the gift of the Light of the World and so is accepted by God. Every individual must feel that God rewards each who diligently seek Him, and as far as this involves independent decision a start must be made from a beginning again in each generation, to acquire the freshness of revelation without which the life will have no full spiritual value. Again, for those obstinate in freewill who remain outside this knowledge and belief, let the prizes of this world crown its own adherents whose longings end with death.

9

A Vicennium, A.D. 80 to 100

In the names of men listed as being with him in Rome, at Colossians 4: 10-14 Paul gives firstly those "of the circumcision" and secondly three who thus appear to be Gentiles: Epaphras, the possible writer of the Epistle to Ephesians, Luke "the beloved physician", and Demas. This last was still with him when he wrote to Philemon (24) but Demas seems to have forsaken Barnabas and Luke some four years later, by 2 Timothy 4:10. Luke is not identical with the Lucius of Cyrene in Acts 13:1, a Jew by Romans 16:21 and Luke did not name himself. Luke's home town may have been Phillippi in Macedonia, and certainly he was valued with gratitude for his loyalty, piety and compassion by Paul (Colossians 4:14 and Philemon 24) and Barnabas (2 Timothy 4:11). If he assembled a gospel document designated as Proto-Luke it antedated Mark, but seems never to have "seen the light of day"; Luke's purpose with it may have been to supply the community in early sixties Rome, the purge of 64 being naturally not foreseen, in which connection within the undeniably ruthless rounding up of the "followers of Chrestus" any book is likely to have been destroyed. We cannot know how much of the Mark came to overlap commonly possessed portions already known to Luke; but if those parts of the Gospel According to St. Luke which are neither in St. Mark nor elsewhere are extracted, it perhaps shows a good percentage of the original Proto-Luke, as the following; all references in St. Luke:

5:1-11, Fishing detail involving Simon.

6:20-49, 11:1-13, 12:1-7, 12:22-34, Elements of Christ's Sermon.

Chapter 7, comprised of five narrative units not given elsewhere.

8:1-3, mention of certain middle-class women.

9:51-62, Details at a Samaritan village.

10:12-16, Certain woes.

10:25-42, Parable of the Good Samaritan, and detail of the Bethany sisters.

11:23-41, 12:35-59, 13:18-33, Sayings in response on occasions.

12:13-15 and 12:16-21, Divided inheritance (in the Egyptian St. Thomas), and parable of the Foolish Farmer.

13:1-17, Reference to Pilate's water project (vide Josephus "Antiq. Book 18.3.2), parable of the Fruitless Fig Tree, and detail of the Impotent Woman.

13:34-35, 19:41-44, Jesus' remorse over Jerusalem.

Chapter 14, Healing of dropsy, parables of Taking the Lowest Place and the Nobleman's Banquet, and teaching on discipleship.

Chapter 15, Parables of the Lost Sheep, Lost Silver, and the Prodigal Son.

Chapter 16, Parable of the Unjust Steward, teaching to Pharisees, and parable of Dives and Lazarus.

17:3-, Lesson of forgiveness sevenfold.

17:7-37, On service, healing of ten lepers, signs of coming of the kingdom, and last days.

18:1-14, Parables of the Unjust judge, and Two Men at Prayer.

19:12-27, Parable of the Ten Talents.

21:12-20, Trauma in witnessing to the world.

22:24-32, Argument on greatest among them, and advice to Simon.

23:5-15, Involvement of Herod Antipas.

23:39-43, Piety of one crucified malefactor.

24:13-35, Narration of two going to Emmaus.

24:36-53, Certain reappearance details, and the Ascension.

A few of the verses here are also presented in the Egpytian Gospel of Sayings ascribed to St. Thomas, doubtless carried orally among the believers, viz. Luke 12:2-3, 12:10, 12:13-14, 13:18-21, 14:16-24, 15:3-7, 16:13, 16:19-31, 17:20-21, 17:34-36. In 2 Timothy 4:9-13 there is indication that Luke and Mark were together, including a reference to books and parchments not very long after Mark had written his gospel account, which Luke might have seen at this intermediate stage between his original collection and his later working of it up to a new published version of the gospel.

The best likelihood seems to be, that when Luke undertook to augment Mark some fifteen years later he brought forward the above-listed material from memory in a process of using Mark's book as his basis, presenting the whole work as he does in alternate Markan and non-Markan columns, so that the passages he took from Mark stand visibly apart. In some places Markan insertions are made within Luke's flow, as in the Passion narrative in Luke 22:14-24:12. If an original purpose back in about 60 had been to commend Christianity to Romans of the patrician upper class, it was carried over into Luke's main project in about the year 80. The Gospel according to St. Luke may reasonably be styled as the Roman Gospel, as it generally sets the Latin characters in a good light as similarly in Acts 23:23-33 where they did the best possible for Paul. Certainly Luke is friendly to the Rome of history, and the Book of Act had been grudging to Judaeo-Christians in comparison. In the dating of St. Luke's gospel a hypothesis that this evangelist used Josephus (who wrote in the nineties) as for instance in referring to Lysanias at Luke 3:1 is unlikely – the reference is to an earlier tetrarch of the same name, and his date of the fifteenth year of Tiberius Caesar (A.D. 28/29)is correct. This is very likely the original beginning of Luke's gospel, following the Preface 1:1-4, because the birth and Infancy narratives are almost certainly not his; the intense Jewishness of these two Chapters would scarcely find Gentile acceptance in the eighties, and it was always Luke's habit to put his sources into his own words. As being a fluent writer there is no prospect of him simply attaching the Chapters untouched and then introducing John the Baptist as the son of Zacharias (3:2) and Jesus by means of a long supposed genealogy (3:23-38) all over again. The St. Luke gospel at this later time was clearly written for Gentile individuals and communities, but no community is visible in Rome from 64 until at least the third decade of the second century; individuals there who were interested in Christianity were upper-crust persons who, on account of their rank, would not have been drawn into the Nero purge such as T. Flavius Clemens or Clement, a joint consul in 95, or Domitilla, a relative of the emperor Domitian (reigned 81-96). Like the St. Matthew author but even more so, Luke polished Mark and amplified the earliest surviving gospel narrative with parables and other Sayings material, and it is largely of this that the projected Proto-Luke seems to have consisted. As something of a literary artist he smoothed the ruggedness existing within the wealth of orally transmitted traditional units for Church circulation according to the developed needs now of the eighties, with an overall result of rather blurring the outlines – which St. John would shortly be sharpening up again – such as to emphasize a broad sympathy focusing on the outcasts and the poor through recording significantly the human gentleness of Christ: it is, besides appealing reasonably to the world of Rome, the most human-oriented of the four gospels and in this, very much a work of its time.

The Gospel according to St. Matthew was written in the mid-eighties, but of its author we have no data. It was not the Apostle Levi Matthew (Mark 2:14-15), because no Apostle would have any need to resort to St. Mark. It is unlikely that these two evangelists knew of each others' projects, for there is no sign of any comparing within the works themselves. The Apostle Matthew is reported to have written a gospel of Sayings in Hebrew which was studied by Origen in the third century and, in the custom of the Ancients of using a pseudepigraphic greater name on a work, it is possible that this author had been associated and desired to use the Apostle's name on his own work to honour it, as someone did for St. Barnabas a few decades later. A second-century father Papias of Hieropolis in his "Exposition of the Dominical Oracles" in about 135 says that "Matthew" (i.e. the Apostle) "compiled the Oracles in Hebrew, and each one interpreted them as he was able". Such document is likely to have been one similar in contents and intent to that in Egpyt ascribed to St. Thomas. Certainly the peculiar detail about getting a coin from a caught fish in order to pay a tax, in Matthew 17:23-26 could surely be drawn only from a tax collector. Inferred from the work itself, this man is likely to have been a Jewish Christian writing at a time when some degree of overlap and conflict in the Christian-Jew split gave an impetus to write in support of what yet remained of the Jewish Church. There are several factors pointing to Syria in the late first century for the place of writing, virtually certain as Antioch: the environment in which it was written was one of syncretism among Greeks, Jews and Romans; a Judaic fiscus temple tax there had to be currently paid to Rome; there was a threat of antinomianism and possibly some development of scandal in the Church. Aside from these environmental concerns there are in this gospel signs of earlier familiarity with Simon Peter either directly or at second hand, and later St. Ignatius as Bishop at Antioch had close knowledge of the St. Matthew book. An apparent regard of primacy for St. Peter is reflected strongly in Matthew as in 16:18-19 which has the appearance of an invented insertion, as does the text in Matthew 23:15 where the verbal violence is not a unit of the Lord Jesus. This piece of text may have been a stimulus for the malediction of Gamaliel II in about 95 "May the Nazarins and heretics be suddenly destroyed and their names obliterated from the Book of life." In 85 the Jewish Church was visibly dying, and for the St. Matthew author it would be a straight forward project to attempt arrangement of the authority of the Lord Jesus to back up direct Jewish ecclesiastical interests of the period, notably against the sect of the Pharisees which by agreement with the Emperor Vespasian had survived in Gaza when Jerusalem was destroyed and other sects as the Sadducees and the Essences had perished.

The Jewish errors down to this time did not go onward but the St. Matthew author, while absorbing about ninety per-cent of St. Mark into his work, made a particular rearrangement of Law and the Pharisees intermixed with the components of Christ's Sermon on the Mount which almost certainly had not originally included that material as given elsewhere variously on other occasions; it furnishes a major instance of contemporary rearranging for local purposes. The gigantic Pharisaic system of tradition mismanagement appears along the horizon in St. Mark already in the sixties, and as a survival beyond the destruction of Jerusalem it may easily have been a factor in the antagonism now existing in the Christian point of view. To some extent the focus on Pharisees but not on Sadducees who were the real villains, in all three synoptic gospels but more especially in St. Matthew is understandable as far as it applied with the evangelists. Against this prospect the fundamental Sermon on the Mount was originally a compact section of faith equipment discourse designed to inaugurate the Lord's disciples comprising the primary group of twelve, given privately to them a few days after the calling of Levi Matthew (Mark 2:14 then 3:13-19) referring to a week with a Sabbath in between. Mark 3:20 says, after the Twelve were listed, that "the multitude came together again." In this action of giving the Sermon, consisting of inaugural guidance little time was lost and none wasted; a close approximation of the original contents may be assembled from the verses appearing in Luke Chapters 6, 11 and 12 parallel with Matthew 5, 6 and 7. The nineteen verses pertaining directly to Pharisaic legal concern given in Matthew 5:17-24, 5:27-28, 5: 31-38 and 5:43 were undoubtedly given, but on various other occasions to Pharisees and often to scribes as well, but not to a lay crowd with fundamental private principles admixed; and it is fair to conclude that this freedom of rearranging renders the St. Matthew as the least reliable of the four gospels of the canon.

In the seasons which are the Lord's who sees the end from the beginning, the gospel account of greatest reliability was now in this similar time written in either the late eighties or early nineties by St. John in a wholly Gentile community at Ephesus. At third generation from this St. Irenaeus, a pupil of St. Polycarp himself a pupil of St. John attested that St. John the Apostle wrote his gospel there, and lived into the reign of the Emperor Trajan (reigned 98-117). Thus John Zebedee was functioning as a really aged man, but old-age memory is often sharp upon details from long years past. This was, and had long been, the best man in the world to bring the essential gospel knowledge into writing: his nearness to Jesus in the days of the holy ministry, his enthusiasm (vide b'ney regesh "son of tumult" Mark 3:17) and his undoubted writing skills all in combination qualified him as the greatest. Why then was his gospel project so long in coming? Often the Lord delays His aid; and with the fantastic human wisdom of hindsight we are able to realize that had the gift been bestowed sooner, the most precious fruit of it would have been lost. With the immortal writings of St. John there is precious fruit indeed.

Knowing intimately the events and conversations in which he long ago had shared, John wrote anecdotally from memory with absolute independence in an easy literary flow forming a book which in all reason is to be taken wholly without question, except that the last Chapter John 21 was not actually by him, and therefore not strictly part of it. The Fourth Gospel signs off fully with John 20:30-31, "These things are written that ye might believe that Jesus is the Christ, the Son of God; and that, believing, ye might have life through His name. (Amen)." The appalling literary jolt into John 21 with relatively mundane material suddenly presented testifies that this Chapter is an addition, with their certificate at 21:24, by the Ephesus brethren who at 21:25 rather uselessly repeat what John had given in his penultimate verse 20:30 about the impossibility of writing all things for the record.

The Ruins of Ephesus, from an 1820 Engraving. This, the home of St. John, remained forgotten for Sixteen Centuries.

Traditionally the Samaritans had looked for a prophet to tell them all things, not for a political king to bring emancipation; and if John had worked for years in that land he must have seen something of the phenomenon wherein realistic opportunists of the Simon Magus type (Acts 8) infected local faith aspirations in operating as cool unabashed liars claiming some spiritual stature. Here at Ephesus in what was really a Greek community the old Jewish and Samaritan expectations or hopes and the charlatans exploiting them did not apply, but there was to some extent a chaos of thought still extending from the Old Greek pagan ideas in religion and theories of philosophy, an environment definitely new to John. The style of his writing, and especially in the Epistle First John where he was able at last to use his own words altogether, shows that he had listened to the cavils of skeptical men and had received good questions from men who were sincere in longing to believe. At first glance it seems possible that he had seen one of the existing gospels, probably St. Mark, and augmented it by adding more details; but this is fairly improbable: for why then would he give certain details again, such as the account of feeding five thousand or that of Jesus' action against cheats in the Jerusalem temple complex? When he wrote his own account John had seen the visions on Patmos and now in a society which in some ways must have surprised him with considerable cultural shock he had reason to lay emphasis upon the sublime aspects, character, work, and assertion of highest claims, of the Lord Jesus. This was done along an excellent narrative background in which John mentioned names without introduction such as John the Baptist (John 1:19) or the Bethany family (11:1) as if his readers already knew of them; but the overall effect, even without consciousness of such design, was that John supplied a valuable completing of Mark.

St. John's gospel is a great gift to all who desire to have a maximum Christian knowledge regarding the events within the ministry of Jesus, and directly from that knowledge, a realization of what it amounts to. At certain points he gives statements useful to the historian which is not available elsewhere, although this also is unlikely to have come within his conscious purpose with the project. By reading "between the lines" we can, as in a more mundane way with the St. Matthew author, glean some knowledge of the contemporary world within which he was writing, and thereby to see some extent of the changes since the earlier decades in the general field of Christendom. Whereas the St. Matthew author was concerned in accounting the great ministry to augment the contemporary interest of Jewish Christians, St. John took in hand the twin prongs, so to speak, of augmenting Gentile understanding in the community with which he was rapidly becoming familiar, and also of positively responding to the negative phenomenon of heretical developments which had by this time grown seriously. On both these points to clarify by means of a word-picture of Jesus of Jesus the Master supplied a substantial sword, and a need for it continued long after John's time. Surely men in the later centuries have no excuse for their schismatic irritabilities and their uncharitable actions in dogmatic intolerance, notably on their confusion upon the nature of Jesus; for John had presented the Lord with absolute clarity, directly from his own intimate personal association and with utter truth, as the Only begotten of the Father standing in full view, and had given the Logos theology by the clearest possible resume with his Aramaic poem at the outset of this gospel project (John 1:1-14). An intention in the project included a component of apologia, a written defence of what the Apostle himself believed, and his faith and belief was immensely strong as would naturally be expected in all the circumstances of his experience and the theological authority deriving from his closeness to Christ Himself. He recounted incidents and parts of teaching and confidential conversations which he thought might best lead others to believe, keeping them in the golden path of truth and orthodoxy.

The fantastic system of Gnosticism, an invented hotch-potch claiming an esoteric spiritual knowledge within an occult mysticism was not yet fully formulated in St. John's time, but there are signs that he was coming up against it by the early nineties. In his substantial assertion of truth against falsehood undertaken by means of the general Epistle First John his old character of what Jesus had nicknamed the son of tumult is visible, as with "Who is a liar but he that denieth that Jesus is the Christ?" in 1 John 2:22, and in this verse the specific term antichrist is reminiscent of the Apocalypse. Some men in his environment had denied or were denying that Jesus Christ had certainly come in the flesh, and any pretence to have spiritual knowledge and favour outside of this marvelous Incarnation was to John, and in all truth, an insufferable form of unbelief. By a testimony of St. Irenaeus, drawing on what he heard from Polycarp, St. John one day discovered that a heresiarch named Cerinthus was within the building at a public bath house he himself intended to use; John then immediately left the building "because this enemy of truth is within". This heretic, originally a Jew, had been teaching an antichristian doctrine that the Son of God did not actually come in the flesh; and as an effective counter to this kind of rubbish John included specifics truly illustrating the marvel that the Word was indeed made flesh "and tabernacled among us" (literally, dwelt in our tents) "and we beheld His glory as of the only begotten" (or, one of a kind) "of the Father" (John 1:14). As this statement ends his opening poem it strongly suggests that the project of this very direct gospel account was deliberately taken up as a practical response to meet the contemporary and local problem posed by all heretical drifting. As an original Christ-ordained Apostle and very likely the only one of them still living, St. John was leading Christians against a composite opposition: on the front a jealous competition by superstitious pagans, on the flank by Jewish bitterness against what they erroneously thought was heresy against their orthodoxy in monotheistic faith of which they supposed they had a perpetual monopoly, and in the rear by the confusion of men professing to belong to Christ but adulterating the faith they purported to receive, by applying an a la carte mish-mash of inventions according to their own taste.

The heresies existing before the destruction of Jerusalem in 70 which are marginally noted by Paul at Colossians 2:8, the author of Ephesians in 5:6 and 6:12, and Barnabas in Titus 1:10-2:1 were of pagan and Jewish inspiration, and probably the more serious phenomenon of Gnosticism developed, slowly at first, after that date and firstly out of the wreckage of apocalyptic Judaism which had already included some speculative hypotheses which must be alien to Christianity. Men with some inclination to form cultic sects were taking from pagan fiction ideas which appealed to them, from the now failed Jewish apocalyptic hope and from Christianity as well; and in the society around John at Ephesus in the last fifteen years of the first century A.D. this heresy of Gnosticism must have been deemed to threaten a serious rivalry to the young Christanity. Besides which it did grow to become larger in the second and third centuries. It is in this background that the original stimulus to St. John's gospel project and his great Epistle should be found. The importance of his writings is seen in later hindsight in that these works above all other Christian accounts provided the only means of eventually defeating just exactly that threat posed by Gnosticism through beating the Gnostics at their own game of theological speculative theorizing, against which the legacy of Paul, Barnabas and Simon Peter likely would not be adequate at their different theological level at which the alien speculative aspect would not be, in their earlier days, attacked: perhaps in a peculiar distorted way we owe it to the Gnostics that they contributed to our equipment by drawing John out. Certainly with his work John built better than he knew in his own time, by supplanting theoretical dreaming to the extent that his holy witness established the truth once and for all at this later time some fifty five years after the departure of the Lord Jesus. Holiness consolidate whereas sin disintegrates, thus although the heretical sects loomed seriously in St. John's immediate view and were then still growing, they were always doomed to fail sooner or later as all human-imagined cults still do, and will. False doctrines growing on the Christian tree like mistletoe on an oak were rooted only in the shallow presumptions of their founders and adherents and lacked the vigorous principles of unassailable truth, whereas John's witness and testimony survived all storms and is permanent. It is a sobering thought here that, without these written works of John Zebedee Christianity in its youth might have drowned in a blunging tide of error so plausible to many in days when many of the best men lacked conviction while the worst were full of passionate intensity. Generally we think of early Christians as suffering mostly from physical persecution, but their faith system was under worse attack doctrinally than we sometimes realize. As with Paul and Simon Peter, let us extract an acme of John, where in this case he gives, as direct connection back to Jesus, actually the Lord's statements transcending the regular practice of preaching.

"In the beginning was the Word, and the Word was with God, and the Word was God. The same was in the beginning with God. All things were made by Him; and without Him was not anything made that was made. In Him was life; and the life was the light of men.

He was in the world, and the world was made by Him, and the world knew Him not. He came unto His own, and His own received Him not. But as many as received Him, to them gave He power to become the sons of God: to them that believe on His name – which were born not of blood, nor of the will of the flesh, nor of the will of man, but of God. And the Word was made flesh, and dwelt among us; and we beheld His glory, the glory as of the only begotten of the Father: full of grace and truth. And of His fullness have we all received, and grace for grace; for the law was given by Moses, but grace and truth came by Jesus Christ.

No man hath seen God at any time; the only begotten Son, which is in the bosom of the Father, He hath declared Him. Verily, verily I say unto thee, Except a man be born of water and of the Spirit, he cannot enter into the kingdom of God. That which is born of the flesh is flesh; and that which is born of the Spirit is spirit. Marvel not that I say, Ye must be rebegotten. The wind bloweth where it listeth and thou hearest the sound thereof, but canst not tell whence it cometh and whether it goeth: so is every one that is born" (begotten again) "of the spirit.

God is a Spirit: and they that worship Him must worship Him in spirit and in truth.

For God so loved the world, that He gave His only begotten Son, that whosoever believeth in His should not perish, but have everlasting life. For God sent His Son into the world not to condemn the world, but that through Him the world might be saved. He that believeth on Him is not condemned; but of him that believeth not in the name of the only begotten Son of God, this is the condemnation, that light is come into the world and men loved darkness rather than light, because their deeds were evil. Verily, verily I say unto you, he that heareth My word and believeth on Him that sent Me, hath everlasting life and shall not come into condemnation, but is passed from death unto life. For, as the father hath life in Himself, so hath he given to the Son to have life in Himself, and hath given Him authority to execute judgment also, because He is the Son of man. Marvel not at this; for the hour is coming, when all that are in the graves shall hear His voice, and shall come forth: they that have done good, unto the resurrection of life; and they that have done evil, unto the resurrection of damnation. And the Father Himself, which hath sent Me, hath borne witness of Me. Ye have neither heard His voice at any time, nor seen His shape. No man can come to Me, except the Father which hath sent Me draw him; and I will raise him up at the last day. For I have not spoken of Myself; but the Father which sent Me, He gave Me a commandment, what I should say and speak. And I know that His commandment is life everlasting. Whatsoever I speak therefore, even as the Father said unto Me, so I speak.

It is written in the prophets, And they shall all be taught of God. Every man therefore that has heard and learned of the Father, cometh to Me. I am the bread of life. Truly I tell you, before Abraham was born, I was alive. I am the light of the World, come into the world that all who believe on Me should not abide in darkness.

I and My Father are One: he that hath seen Me hath seen the Father. It is the spirit that quickens – the flesh profiteth nothing. The words that I speak unto you are spirit and life, for I am the resurrection and the life. He that believeth in Me, though he were dead, yet shall he live. Because I live, ye shall live also. A new commandment I give unto you, that ye love one another. As I have loved you, that ye also love one another. By this shall all people know that ye are my disciples, if ye have love one to another".

Of the character named Clement of Rome who wrote a long letter from that city to the Corinthian Christian community in the mid-nineties, practically nothing is known. In first-century Rome an early association of Jewish Christians joined by St. Paul at the end of the fifties, had been blotted out in the days of Nero and no other such community is known of until the time of Marcion in the 130's and Anecitus in the 150's. The Flavian dynasty of emperors after Nero, that is, Vespasian, Titus and Domitian were, apart from Titus' short reign of only two years (79-81) unfriendly to the Christian movement, although not to any extent raising a record of direct or wide persecution. A policy was begun of treating Christians as outlaws liable to death on confession of the name of Christ Jesus, but in any case Rome regarded the Christians merely as Jews of a particular sect or cult regardless of nationality: hatred of what Tacitus called "mischievous superstition" was the mainspring behind Roman opposition as far as it then went – it was not a specific manifestation of antichrist. Further, at the beginning of Vespasian's reign in 69 the Judean war was in full spate, and clearly when Jerusalem was destroyed in 70 there was not scope for any Christian development in Rome. In the appalling reign of Domitian (81-96) the period was packed with wars which turned this emperor into a cruel tyrant to the extent that even among his own relatives Flavius Clemens (husband of Domitilla) was executed and Domitilla (his niece) was banished, as they being persons "guilty of atheism and Jewish manners"; certainly any idea of Christianity flourishing in the Roman Empire must be far distant in the future. Domitian met his death at the hands of a freedman, Stephanus, in a plot by the empress Domitia on 18 September 96. It was crude and rough, yet even in these circumstances a knowledge and interest in Christianity had survived in individuals among the higher classes in Rome, persons who being outside the pale of Delatorre intrigues of politics, were not attacked or persecuted. Evidently such persons were living there when Ignatius wrote in a style of entreaty in 114 on his way to martyrdom in the city, that they should not impede his path to martyrdom; clearly he regarded whoever were the Roman recipients of his letter to be able to influence the secular power. It is quite likely that in the nineties Clement of Rome was such a member of the privileged class. But the alternative idea that this man was, as a disciple of Peter, the third Bishop of Rome, is bunk.

The letter to Corinth regularly designated as First Clement (because a spurious homily dating in the third or fourth decade of the second century was also claimed as Second Clement) existed in an early Latin translation which may be the oldest item of Christian literature in that language. As to the occasion for this missive, it is possible that in some areas along the Mediterranean Jewish Christians now in the nineties were being excommunicated within the Christian-Jew split which by this time had become practically total. Originally there had been a preference for outreach to Jews, then Gentiles were welcomed as being not bound under any Jewish tenets, and a Jewish identity was maintained aside from the Gentiles in the widening Christian field. But it was a faith revolution, as the men involved at the time must have been aware; and if Judaic adherence as a cultural or nationality label was applied anywhere in this Christendom now overwhelmingly become of a Gentile population, it would get no particular and sympathetic support. By Malachi 1:11 in inspired prophecy, "My name shall be great among the heathen, saith the Lord of hosts" a text used in Hebrews 8:10-13 on a new people of God raised up in a new covenant, this must constitute the model faced by the Jewish leaders based in their Jamnia Academy, as the reign of Domitian ended. But these leaders such as Gamaliel II or Rabbi Akiba ben Joseph found texts like Matthew 23:15: "Woe unto you, scribes and Pharisees, hypocrites! For ye compass sea and land to make one proselyte, and when he is made, ye make him twofold more the child of hell than yourselves, "and if so finding must have been shocked at it. The contemporary Jews of the surviving Pharisee sect could not make comparisons sufficiently to realize the very high likelihood that these words were not originally spoken by the Lord Jesus at all. In the gospels the same matter given at Mark 12:38-40 does not mention either Pharisees or the making of proselytes; and certainly by the time of Clement's writing in about the year 95 adequate possibilities for divisions of within Christendom had accumulated.

The writer was well versed in the Septuagint version of the Old Testament Scriptures, citing freely from all parts of it, which suggests either Jewish nationality or a deep connection with others of it, in Clement. He was acquainted with Paul's letter to the Corinthians and of course with that to Romans and he quoted in Clem. 36:2-5 directly from Hebrews 1:3-7 and 1:13, itself quoted from Psalms 104:4, 2:7-8 and 110:1. Significantly – from the historian's point of view – there is no trace of Petrine influence in Clement; had the Apostle Simon Peter been teaching and living in Rome thirty or forty years previously, at least a moderate degree of signs of him must have shown through. Clement's remarks on the subject of dissention reflect a close parallel in James, especially 4:1-11 which had been a letter to the Jewish Church but not to Rome, but he refers his readers in Clem. 47 to Paul at 1 Corinthians 3:1-9 using the names Cephas and Apollos which appear in 1 Corinthians 3:22. If merely local quarrelling among the Corinthian brethren had been the whole issue, it is difficult to see this as the driving reason for the letter by a patrician Roman nobleman, possibly Jew: and had it been the primary reason, more would be seen of it in the letter. A reference to calamities recently suffered at Rome (Clem 6 and 7) is likely to be registering a concern about the hostile activities of Domitian in the late eighties and early nineties, where the writer quotes examples further in Clem 47 of Gentiles in historical actions of self-sacrifice for the good of the State: those who cause schism in Christendom should clear out rather than remain to disturb the peace. Along the middle of his letter Clement is apprehensive that love to fellow men will soon wax cold, and probably he had either seen or heard of irrefutable evidence of such thing on a serious scale. In Clem. 33, "What must we do then, my brothers? Should we relax our efforts at well-doing, and cease to exercise Christian love? God forbid that we, at least, should ever come to such a pass". This strongly reflects James from a generation earlier. Again from Hebrews he notes that all things are naked and open before the eyes of the Lord of the ordered universe (Hebrews 4:13), enjoins obedience to the powers that be (Hebrews 13:17) and requires female silence in the Church (12 Corinthians 14:34 but also 1 Timothy 2:11-12) in Clement 21. By Clement we are enjoined to cast away injurious negative attitudes in a piety operating practically in that the indulging of such attitudes is surely abhorrent to God; indeed it is fair to ask, upon whom does the indulging of permissive and indiscipline's confer any favour? With St. James he took the view that "We are saved by faith, but our faith must adorn itself with (Good) works if we would be followers of God" – clearly this was not a view drawn from Paul in the eighth of Romans.

In the last two decades of the first century A.D. there are thus three main dealings in different Christian base areas. Firstly at Ephesus which very likely represents Asia Minor as a whole, where St. John was a main instrument against contemporary heresies which appear to have posed a major threat; secondly in West Greece where Corinth was a principal centre, a region where probably Jews of any Christian profession had been cut dead by the resurgence (vide 1 Corinthians 3) of some aspects of pride or envy; and thirdly at Antioch in Syria a need had arisen to combat tendencies to antinomianism and there was a parallel desire to accommodate the Jewish Christians who by the nineties seem to have had no other home. Across this general scene St. John is the one extraordinary and powerful ray of light. He speaks to all and sundry with high enthusiasm and without any hint of pecking order, exactly in the manner of those first days back in 33; others may have buckled under pressures of change down the decades, but not this man who had been closest to the Spring of the grand faith and had been blessed with isolation and preservation for so many years, and to whom had been marvelously vouchsafed the visions on Patmos. Near the end of his long life he brought a revelation of the light, life and love of the Eternal Father in communion with every believing individual as His child: not by an effluence of some unknowable Being, but by the personal, eternal, divine and incarnate Word of God. His General Epistle of a spiritual parental authority vested in this last of Christ's Apostles on earth supplements all of the gospel accounts, and perhaps was undertaken as a letter in deliberation of farewell. It is pastoral rather than polemic in character, and was written after the Gospel according to St. John; where he warns his readers to test the spirits (1 John 4:1-3) it is certain that they already had such capacity in their possession. With his gospel project John had been meeting Jews or judaizers who denied the messiahship of the Lord Jesus, and later near the end of his life he met, with the great Epistle, heretics who having half received Christianity distorted it by denying the Incarnation of Christ. John saw that our spiritual welfare needed a bulwark against varieties of antichristian error, and he provided it. On early second-century testimony it is said that when at last he was dying near the year 100 St. John continually urged the brethren around him to cultivate love one to another, over and over again. When asked "Why do you say this, and nothing else?" he replied, "Because if you do this, nothing else is needed".

10

Early Second Century

In a form of survey across Christianity's first six and a half decades down to A.D. 100 the general view is, that the full positive reaction to the Resurrection event which had brought immediate realization of Jesus' holy ministry into men's minds and hearts in 33 was not sustained in its natural-from-supernatural high level in them after the early or mid-fifties, and certainly between the death of St. Paul in 64 and the re-emergence of St. John at Ephesus in about 79 or 80. In the years between Simon Peter, Barnabas, Mark, Luke and Timothy were, as salient Christians, obliged to cope with two phenomena: a comparative and perhaps inevitable cooling to lukewarmness in overall faith conviction across the wide geographically separate clutch of small believing communities – where no new Paul was produced, and the ever present backcloth of opposition from Jews and pagans, plus the heresies which after about 60 began to develop from sources belonging to both.

Particularly with St. John among the Asia Minor Gentiles there was a revival, and posterity owes this greatest of the Apostles an overwhelming debt for his provision of the highest possible spiritual witness of great clarity and permanence. Into the second century A.D. this geographic region was really the site of Christendom; perhaps it is not too much to claim that this was where the Christian System was saved. Certainly it was eventually to be the first Christian Roman emperor's choice of location for a new imperial capital: Palestine, Syria, West Greece and Rome were not candidates for the primal centre of the Christian world, though at the time when St. John departed this life such thing was all invisibly away in the future. At this same time the Jewish Church was dying, and it is likely that efforts by Vespasian and Domitian against Jewish Christians had been a large factor in contributing to that death; according to Hegesipus as preserved by Eusebius, the Emperor Domitian became afraid of a messianic uprising among the Jews and in consequence ordered that the descendants of David be put to death. The Jewish Church left such documents as the Didache and the Shepherd of Hermes, but nothing is known of it beyond the death of its second leader Symeon in about 104, apart from a heretical sect of Ebionites which survived into the third century but, as heresy, was of no general or external consequence.

From the letters of St. Ignatius it seems certain that Antioch sought to find strength for survival in a method of consolidation rubbing off from the world, so to speak, through leadership authority: "The Bishop must stand firm as an anvil when it is struck" (Ign. Polycarp 3). However, in Asia Minor the communities were still gathering as they always had, for simple procedures of worship and religious association in the manner of the first decades. This is evidenced by a fragment of Roman correspondence in 112, where nothing is yet indicated of a salient community leader identified in the ever vigilant Roman eyes. As proconsul in the districts of Pontus and Bithynia in northern Asia Minor Pliny the Younger wrote a letter to Emperor Trajan in which he noted a local falling away of Roman pagan worship, and indicated that he had probed into what the local Christians were up to. He had subjected two female slaves to torture, but had not been able to find anything illegal under Roman law, in the practices at Christian gatherings. He remarked that they normally met together at dawn on a certain day of the week (which we may take as Sunday) to sing a hymn of praise to Christ their God, and solemnly swore to abstain from theft and adultery, never to break their word, and to withhold no property entrusted to their keeping, after which they separated and later reassembled for a simple meal (the eucharist). Those who refused to abjure Christ and worship the emperor instead were executed; Pliny then asked for further instructions for any other action to be taken. In replying, Trajan approved of what had so far been done, and gave direction that the Christians were not to be specifically searched out but, if any refused to recant on information brought against them measures of severity were to be taken in such cases. By this it seems certain that any persecution of the Christians in these districts would arise as a result of individual informers against them: that significantly it was not official as a deliberate policy in this reign, a period in which such thing is not noted elsewhere. Pliny the younger had been sent as legatus Augusti to reorganize the disorderly province of Bithynia in about 110, and he died there in office soon after the correspondence about Christians had been done. His action of referring the matter of them back to Trajan may have arisen only out of concern as to how far that Community might be a factor in the conditions requiring the reorganizing not necessarily from any perceived and isolated need for a purge against it.

It was only two years after this that in 114 Ignatius wrote his seven known letters. This date is known with certainty, because the bishop was brought before Trajan at Antioch when the Emperor was there in connection with a war against Parthia, when he required the Armenian King Parthomasiris to lay his crown before Him. He was evidently at Antioch for some time, since in the following year he narrowly escaped death in the earthquake of 115; but he died on his homeward journey en route for Rome, at Selinus in Cilicia in August 114. Since he apparently had no official policy of persecuting Christians as such, his confining of Ignatius for martyrdom involves some individual reason. From the Bishop's letters it is clear that he was a strenuous advocate of authority in principle and practice; in this, it is likely that Ignatius Bishop of Antioch (itself a major city in the Roman

Empire) was considered by the Roman authorities to be something of a social figurehead of a position already grown to some size, in which he might sooner or later amount potentially to a political threat. To allow harmless-looking gatherings was one thing, but to tolerate a militant-looking alien leader was something else. It was as a cultic ringleader, not as a Christian, that Ignatius was singled out to answer to Trajan; and the fact that they bothered to transport him to Rome for execution strongly suggests that the Romans regarded him as a figure of some importance or possible consequence: in the ordinary way a sentence of death would be carried out in the place of judgement. Why take him to distant Rome if this was mere persecution of the local Christians? We have no record or tradition of any other interference with the Christian community at Antioch at this time; and although no doubt that community felt the loss of their leader, it is not automatic that they would be in turmoil as a result of his removal for martyrdom. In his letter to St. Polycarp Ignatius requested that a delegate or delegation be sent to Antioch (Ign. Polycarp 7) which discloses a degree of concern for his former flock, but at the same time affirms that the community had not been destroyed. His letters contain two main themes: 1. An insistence upon Episcopacy with the bishop as the one and only centre of vested authority, and 2. A doctrinal warning position against the Docetic heresy and other heretical tendencies from Jewish origin, which were currently serious at the time. In the collection of his letters we have the earliest sure reference to the method of Church government by the mechanism of threefold order in bishops, presbyters and deacons as the assumed essential means of securing unity.

Of these letters only that to St. Polycarp at Smyrna was to a single individual. How well Ignatius knew any of the receiving communities is not to be guessed at, except that the general tone of the letters suggests that he had not been intimate with any of them, and possibly regarded himself as salient, in a degree of what would in later centuries be understood as a papal figure.

He was acquainted with certain important names in the Christian connection, perhaps including one or more names among the contemporary few upper-class patricians in Rome such as Clement, people there who were interested in what they knew of the Christian doctrine ultimately down from St. Paul in their city. Certainly he had a definite destination of known recipient to which to write, and where he entreats people at Rome to refrain from using an influence towards any reprieve of his fate (Ign. Romans 6) it was not a letter addressed to a plebian mob of ordinary folk. The letter to Rome does not greet any bishop or other Christian leader there, but in some contrast it is of an altogether general character which, unlike all the other letters does not touch upon either Episcopacy or Docetism and is thereby isolated within the collection in its spirit, contents and purpose. In fine, in his Roman Letter he was not writing to a church or a specific leader, and here he had concern only for his own process in which he desired to be "unhindered from receiving the pure light" in a martyrdom in which he expressed the hope that the beasts to be tearing him "would be prompt". Ignatius was a champion of Orthodoxy who would proceed to all extremities to protect the flock against currents dangers of powerful judaizing cultic and speculative tendencies (Ign. Magnesians 8, 9 and 10 and Ign. Philadelphians 6 to 9); but really he was a martyr not to the sacred cause of Christ exactly, but rather to the Episcopalian ideal. In sharing with Paul an intensely personal gift of communicating in words the passion of his convictions, he seems at the same time to have embodied credal formulae which in the record of the second of Acts were Petrine affirming Jesus' Davidic line of descent which elsewhere appear only with Mark (10:47-48) but mostly Matthew (9:27, 12:23 and 15:22) in the gospels. In the letter to Ephesus Ignatius gave a more developed note on the Star of Bethlehem (Ign. Ephesus 19) than that in Matthew 2:2, which suggests that some early source of knowledge in this unit was available to him independently of the St. Matthew author from whom however, he quoted as for example Matthew 3:15 at

Ign. Smyrneans 1:1, Matthew 12:33 at Ign. Ephesians 14:2, Matthew 19:12 at Ign. Smyrneans 6:1, and Matthew 10:16 at Ign. Polycarp 2:2.

It is virtually certain that Ignatius did not know the Apostle St. John personally, for in the Ephesus letter there is no reference to him at all. However, he may have seen the Gospel according to St. John, because there are several parallels of Johannine phrase visible in the letters, as "the Spirit knowing whence he comes and whither he goes" (Ign. Philadelphians 7:1/John 3), Christ as the door (Ign. Philadelphians 9:1/John 15), "the living water" and "the bread of God" (Ign. Romans 7:2-3/John 4 and 6). Yet at some points he was certainly indistinct on the Logos theology of St. John, as where in Ign. Ephesians 18:2 the word or logos is claimed to date only from the Incarnation, and the pre-existence of the Eternal Son of John 1:1-14 with the Father, is not strongly upheld: "The generation of Jesus Christ in Divine dispensation manifest through Mary after the seed of David but by the Holy Spirit" was Ignatius' theological view, dangerously limited if the heresies abounding, the splendid effort of St. John to counter them, and the now matured Christian-Jew split are considered as circumstances of the time. Elsewhere the coupling of Mary in the house and lineage of David is applied to Joseph as of a secular understanding. In Ignatius there is more of the developed tradition at Antioch from Simon Peter than of the brilliant revival from St. John at Ephesus. His letters are a writing of a mature man not greatly aged and certainly not a youth, and his age at the time of his martyrdom might be guessed at about sixty, thus born in the fifties of the first century. Two weak "traditions" regarding him, viz. that he had been a child whom Jesus took upon His knee, and that he had been a pupil of St. John, have no basis whatever for credence.

Polycarp however, was originally a pupil of St. John, according to a direct testimony of St. Irenaeus in a letter written to his fellow pupil of Polycarp, Florinus, in 177. Of the accepted date of 155 Polycarp was martyred at Smyrna, a fact attested in a letter from there to another community at Philomelium. His age at the time is given as eighty-six which, even if only approximate sets his birth at about 70 A.D. so he would be in his twenties when in the company of St. John. In the testimony of Irenaeus: "I distinctly remember the incidents of that time better than events of recent occurrence; for the lessons received in childhood, growing with the growth of the soul, become identified with it so that I can tell the very place in which the blessed Polycarp used to sit when he discoursed, and his goings out and his comings in, and his manner of life, and his personal appearance, and the discourse which he held before the people, and how he would describe his intercourse with John and the rest of those who had seen the Lord, and how he would relate their words. And whatsoever things he had heard from them about the Lord and about His miracles and about His teaching. Polycarp, as having received them from eyewitnesses of the life of the Word, would relate together in accordance with the Scriptures. To these things I used to listen at the time with attention, by God's mercy which was bestowed upon me, noting them down not on paper but in my heart; and constantly, by the grace of God, I ruminate upon them faithfully. And I can testify in the sight of God, that if that blessed and apostolic elder had heard anything of this kind, he would have cried out and stopped his ears, and would have said after his wont, "O good God, for what times hast Thou kept me, that I should endure these things!" and would have fled from the very place where he was sitting or standing when he heard such words. And indeed, this can be shown from his letters, which he wrote either to the neighboring churches for their confirmation, or to certain of the brethren for their warning and exhortation. "– it is unclear whether by "apostolic elder" Irenaeus means Polycarp or St. John; but the two short existing letters Second and Third John (this last doubtful as to authorship) give no substantiation here for the Apostle, and it is better to assume the revered letter writer to have been Polycarp in days more recent to Irenaeus than those of John. From the time of St. John until near the end of the second century a struggle between Christianity, situated very largely in the East and Gnosticism, was a matter of life and death. Irenaeus does not indicate what was the heresy with doctrine to have "heard anything of this kind", but clearly they were still up against a long familiar phenomenon of heresy in the fourth quarter of the second century, because in reference to heretical words Irenaeus used the present tense.

As having been an immediate disciple of St. John, Polycarp was apparently the principal agent carrying the Christian torch forward from that Apostle whom Jesus loved, to the middle of the second century. His ministry was long. Probably his home town was Smyrna, to which he would thus return on or after St. John's death to naturally lead the Christian community there. Who then, would be leading now at Ephesus? Frequent contacts with the Pastoral Epistles appearing in Polycarp's letter to the church at Philippi, written soon after Ignatius strongly suggest Timothy as being still there, but it is a particular source of irritation that the existing records show nothing definite of Timothy after the midseventies when the Hebrews author noted his release from a captivity at some place not named. It is further probable that of the Polycarp to Philippi letter only the last portion comprising Chapters 13 and 14 as presented, date as original – the larger part of it was designed to stand against the later heresy of Marcion in the 130's and belongs to a time when all four gospels were in possession and use. The dual purpose of the original as a short letter was, to ask for anything known of Ignatius after he had passed through Philippi on the way to Rome, also for copy of any further letter to add to those already collected by St. Polycarp, and to confirm that arrangements were actually being made to meet Ignatius' request for delegations from the communities of Asia Minor and Macedonia to go to Antioch. In such early days it is unlikely that Polycarp would be immersed in the officers-and-other-ranks aspect of Episcopal organization, because the private letter of Ignatius to him was of a kind indicating some urgency toward pastoral guidance: it was not a letter from one bishop to another in the regular sense. The Smyrnean leader would be grounded essentially in the common democratic flock revering one Lord on a life-saving basis that love is unity and faith is the opposite of fear, the doctrine on the practical side flowing recently from St. John the Divine. They were slowly developing a strap-and-buckles machinery to fight heretical errors, thereby in effect shoving this holy doctrine aside when really if developed alternatively it would be the best means of defence. However, the threats and difficulties confronting the second century cannot be appreciated at a desk of the twenty-first, and it would be uncharitable to expect perfection even in the saints of the Church in any era. Fairly late in his life Polycarp had at least two pupils in Irenaeus and Florinus, and he visited Rome where a Christian community had at last been re-established, to confer with its leader Anicetus about a correct time in the year for celebrating the Passion. These leaders did not agree on this time but agreed to differ. The Easter Controversy was fated to become a pain in the Church later, but the time was not yet come for ceremonial trifles to split Christendom: that was for the fourth century and onwards. Perhaps their evident collective forbearance was rooted in the environment of being drawn close around a water hole, so to speak, in those days of serious struggle against widespread heresies of a kind which, as proclaiming Christ's humanity to be mere apparition, focused on intellectual speculations with a sensuality carried to extreme mysticism. Orthodox Christianity had enough on its hands without finding any in-fighting to do, and in this same visit Polycarp was confronted by the heresiarch Marcion at Rome, a leader there of an ascetic school. Marcion was not a Gnostic but was influenced by that heresy as being somewhat mixed in his ideas; an ardent adherent of St. Paul, he made up his own canon of writings he deemed acceptable in a process in which he rejected all of the Old Testament altogether, and stripped out all Jewish connotations from the gospels, retaining only the Gospel according to St. Luke minus the birth and infancy narratives. As purging his estimated canon of all "accretions and Jewish interpolations" this man may have been a prime influence behind the contemporary desire at Rome to get away from the time of the Jewish Passover in celebrating Easter. Irenaeus notes that when Polycarp and Marcion met, the latter asked for acknowledgement, on which Polycarp replied, "Acknowledge you? Aye! I acknowledge the first-born of Satan".

What started the persecution at Smyrna in 155 is not known, but it seems to have erupted in the local pagan mob and was not due to any official action by the Roman authorities in the benign reign of Marcus Aurelius. Here Polycarp went to his death with the full dignity of old age, after a lifetime of good Christian service as certainly a worthy successor to St. John which kept the Asia Minor Region central to the faith for at least the rest of the century. By his flock he was regarded as a saint, whether officially canonized or not, and the anniversary of his martyrdom was celebrated in churches throughout that whole area; like St. Athanasius in a later century he was to be known as a champion of Orthodoxy, which would undoubtedly refer to his long service achievement generally in success against heretical attacks rather than to the circumstances only around the fatal persecution which was merely pagan as described in the Smyrnean letter to Philomelium. The fact that eleven Christians were thrown to wild beasts in the stadium at Smyrna before Polycarp was himself arrested suggests that the orgy took place on an occasion of one of their emperor-worship festivals. Polycarp's summary of Christianity embraced faith, hope and love, coming directly from St. John: "Love towards God, Christ, and our neighbor". Although the persecution was simply mob-driven Polycarp was nevertheless brought before the Roman proconsul as an "atheist", who pressed him to swear by Caesar from which he would be released. In reply to this, the bishop said, "Eighty-six years have I served Christ, and He hath never done me wrong; and how can I blaspheme my King who saved me?" Thereupon the mob testified to the importance of this salient Christian and the geographical significance of their land in Christendom in their shouting "This is the teacher of Asia, the father of the Christians, the puller down of our gods, who teaches numbers not to sacrifice nor worship the gods".

Another champion of Orthodoxy but less well known was the writer of the Epistle of Barnabas. This work could not be by St. Barnabas himself, because it is evidently dated at about 120 from the reference in it to Hadrian's rebuilding of the temple at Jerusalem re-named Aelia Capitolina, the reference at Barnabas 16 being in the present tense, but it was customary for a disciple to append a master's name on a work of their own, as tribute and memorial. This work was not included in the New Testament canon perhaps principally because it was not written in the first century, but it is close to the author of the Pastoral Epistles and generally shows the instruction contained in First and Second Timothy. If St. Timothy is guessed as the author he would in 120 be in his mid-seventies; the Epistle also has quite close affinities with the Epistle of Peter and the Book of Hebrews.

In the background of his Epistle was the reign of Hadrian, a man with a sense of humour and one tolerant of all religions since he did not owe allegiance to any. In 122-23 he wrote to the proconsul of Asia Minicus Fundanus a rescript enjoining moderation in dealing with Christians. A copy of this rescript was appended by Justin Martyr to Justin's First Apology in about 150. Hadrian was not supportive of paganism, and he finally put an end to Jewish revolts when, after some revolts by this virtually ungovernable people in Cyprus, Cyrene and Egypt had already been put down near the end of Trajan's reign in 117 he crushed the more serious revolt of Bar Kochba in 135. Certainly the cruelties inflicted on Christians by Bar Kochba as an ally of the Jewish leader Rabbi Akiba ben Joseph, who hated the Christian gospel, were a factor at last alerting the Roman Raj to the difference between Jews and Christians – it was eventually aware that the Christian following was not merely another Jewish sect, and this may have paved the way for a lighter Roman touch regarding Christianity in the reigns between Hadrian and the first Roman Christian reign of Constantine beginning in 312. When in 134 Jericho had been destroyed and Bethlehem reduced, Jews were barred from Aelia Capitolina and many were sold into slavery but a Christian bishop was allowed in that city. Within the purely secular intentions of Hadrian the savage detestation of the Jews not only for Rome but in parallel with their hatred of the Christians, was swept away in this reign. A denial of truth in faith destroyed their spiritual inheritance infinitely more than racial bigotry in the world as a whole destroyed their inbred bodies, down the centuries, of this unfortunate people of Jewry who would have acted and fared just the same if Christianity had not existed. With the author of Barnabas the ancient Scriptures are seen as fundamentally behind Christianity – unlike the queer case of Marcion- but any idea of continuing a regard of Judaism as a privileged and chosen religion before all other people had become a joke.

The intent of the Book of Hebrews might have been to serve either to persuade Gentile Christians to more greatly accept the fact of Christ as belonging to the Judaic culture, or to accommodate Jewry in general to harmonise a better coexistence with the Christian system which believed certainly that the Messiah originally promised to the nation of the Jews, foreign to Gentiles, had already come. But the Jews, continuing to assume themselves to be a race apart, went on believing then, as now, that He was not come yet; and they will have a long wait. From Ignatius it is clear that the judaizing faced in the sixties (vide letter to Titus) was more seriously widespread in the East in the early second century, as his two themes were connected in that an organizing of strong leadership was seen as the method of dealing with judaizing tendencies as, among other shortcomings such as the Docetic heresy of denial, these threatened the church communities in several locations. At Antioch, where Ignatius may have been resident since the early seventies and may have briefly known Simon Peter and been present when inevitably that Apostle's leadership had been replaced, that community did not put their trust in the practical principle of dependence in education for democratic unity of the flock whose strength of faith and belief would more effectively guard them against all extremities of the world; in effect it was a veering away from the teachings of Jesus and a corresponding bias towards worldly solutions, and Ignatius' sentence "The Bishop must stand firm as an anvil when it is smitten" to Polycarp at Smyrna, clearly says as much. Only a few years after the writing of the Ignatius letters, perhaps six, the Epistle of Barnabas was written in a project scope which might, as with the Book of Hebrews, be intended to accommodate Jews with Christians, but applying a different method. Is this another possible link of Timothy from Hebrews 13:23? One of the differences here from the seventies when Hebrews had been written was that, in this later time amid the era of Jewish revolts against Rome in 116-134 Jewish scholars or scribes were raising new literature, the Misha and a new translation of the Old testament books by Aquila of Pontus to supplant the Greek Septuagint version which had been in regular use for a couple of centuries. This undertaking was contemporary in the first two decades of the second century, and it is possible that the Epistle of Barnabas may have further been intended as a counterblast to the Jewish literary effort. The writer was at pains to explain Christian meanings out of copiously quoted Old Testament texts to a degree suggesting an intention for Jewish readers rather than Gentile Christians to whom the ancient Scriptures would normally be less familiar. Early second-century Pontus, the region which for some purposes included Bithynia was full of diasporic Jews, but it is not known whether Aquila was writing actually there, or elsewhere. Marcion also came from Pontus, and is said to have been a wealthy shipowner there; and as an incidental, his peculiar distortion discloses Roman Christianity to have been, in the early second century, in a state of extreme infancy. Taken as a whole, the Epistle of Barnabas reflects a reappearance of the preaching methods of the secondary Apostles Barnabas and Paul in the days when their early outreach was to Jews in various synagogues as described in Acts 13:14-41, but this whole business of teaching the advent of the new faith system by bringing it out of the old is perhaps most directly instanced at the opening of Barnabas 13: "But let us see if this (Christian) people is the heir, or the former, and if the covenant belongs to us or to them. Hear ye now what the scripture saith concerning the people. Isaac prayed for Rebecca his wife, because she was barren; and she conceived. Furthermore also, Rebecca went forth to enquire of the Lord; and the Lord said to her, 'Two nations are in thy womb, two peoples in thy belly; and the one people shall surpass the other, and the elder shall serve the younger' (Genesis 25:23). You ought to understand who was Isaac, who Rebecca, and concerning what persons He declared that this people should be greater comparatively". The writer then adds a similar case, that of Joseph with his father Jacob concerning Joseph's sons Manasseh and Ephraim with the elder and younger reversed, from Genesis 48:8-22. Barnabas 18, which is a short Chapter, consists in a reference to "the ways of doctrine and authority, the one of light and the other of darkness", seen elsewhere in the Dead Sea Scrolls belonging to a library of the sect of Essenes with which the Christians are generally unlikely to have been acquainted; substantial references to this same subject then comprise the next two Chapters of the Epistle.

This work drew freely upon Old Testament scriptural extracts for Christian-Jew explanatory purposes in which the writer often quotes rather inaccurately as if he were making the quotes from memory, albeit as a man thoroughly well read in them as, by Second Timothy 3:14-16 Timothy was, from an early age. This writer had been trained on the Septuagint Scriptures and had seen the development of the Christian-Jew split during his own time. A few of his quotations are not found in our Old Testament, as for instance: "For the prophet says, 'Who shall understand the parable of the Lord, except him who is wise and prudent, and who loves his Lord?" Again, "And Abraham circumcised ten, and eight, and three hundred men of his household"; also Barnabas gives a detailed resume of the Jewish ceremonial of Azazel, the sacrificing of a goat for sins but here using a heifer calf, all of which is not generally found. On the other hand the writer gives a good deal of text in the non-scriptural parts showing close affinity with the Pastoral Epistles, mostly those to Timothy, as follows:

In the Epistle of Barnabas	In Timothy and Titus
I rejoice because ye have received the engrafted spiritual gift.	I thank God, whom, I serve from my forefathers with pure conscience, that without ceasing I have remembrance of thee in my prayers; greatly desiring to see thee, that I may be filled with joy, when I call to remembrance the unfeigned faith that is in thee,(2 Tim. 1:3-5a).
The Lord hath accompanied me in the way of righteousness.	The Lord stood with me, and strengthened me; that by me the preaching might be fully known. (2 Tim. 4:17a)
I write unto you in order that, with your faith, ye might have perfect knowledge. (These three units in Barn. 1)	But be thou an example of the believers, in word, in conversion, in charity, in spirit, in faith, in purity. (1 Tim. 4:12b).
The days are evil, and Satan possesses the power of this world.	This know also, that in the last days perilous times shall come... of men denying the power of godliness... ever learning and never able to come to the knowledge of the truth. (2 Tim. 3:1 plus 3:2a, 3:5b and 3:7)

A sacrifice to God is a broken spirit; a smell of sweet savour to the Lord is a heart that glorifieth Him that made it.

(These two units in Barn 2)

Let us utterly flee from all the works of iniquity (Barnabas 4).

Thou shalt not join thyself to such men as are ungodly to the end. (Barnabas 10).

Let us not give loose reins to our soul, that it should have power to run with sinners and the wicked, lest we become like them.

The whole time of your faith will profit you nothing unless now in this wicked time we also withstand coming sources of danger.

If a man purge himself, he shall be a vessel unto honour, sanctified, and meet for the Master's use, and prepared unto ever good work. Flee also youthful lusts; but follow righteousness, faith, charity, peace, with them that call on the Lord out of a pure heart. (2 Tim. 2:21-22).

Perverse disputing of men of corrupt minds, and destitute of the truth, supposing that gain is godliness: from such withdraw thyself. (1 Tim. 6:5)

And they shall turn away their ears from the truth, and shall be turned unto fables. But watch thou in all things, endure afflictions... make full proof of thy ministry. (2 Tim. 4:4-5).

All that will live godly in Christ Jesus shall suffer persecution; evil men and seducers shall wax worse and worse, deceiving and being deceived. But continue thou in the things which thou hast learned and hast been assured of ... that from a child thou hast known the holy Scriptures. (2 Tim. 3:12-15a)

That the Black One may find no means of entrance, let us flee from every vanity.

Coming together in one place, make common enquiry concerning what tends to your general welfare.

Each will receive as he has done: if he is righteous, his righteousness will precede him. If he is wicked, the reward of wickedness is before him.

Take heed, lest we should fall asleep in our sins and the wicked prince acquiring power over us, should thrust us away from the kingdom of the Lord.

(These seven units in Barn. 4.)

But foolish and unlearned questions avoid, knowing that they do engender strifes. And the servant of the Lord must not strive, but be gentle unto all men, apt to teach, and patient; that they may recover themselves out of the snare of the devil, who are taken captive by him at his will. (2 Tim. 2:23-24 and 2:26).

Them that sin rebuke before all, that others also may fear. I charge thee before God, and the Lord Jesus Christ, and the elect angels, that thou observe these things without preferring one before another, doing nothing by partiality. (1 Tim. 5:20-21)

Some men's sins are open before land, going before to judgement; and some they follow after. Likewise also the good works of some are manifest beforehand; and they that are otherwise cannot be hid. (1 Tim. 5:24-25).

Moreover, he must have a good report of them which are without; lest he fall into reproach and the snare of the devil. (1 Tim. 3:7).

Behold again, Jesus who was manifested both by type and in the flesh is not the son of man, but the Son of God. (Barnabas 12).	And without controversy great is the mystery of godliness: God was manifest in the flesh, justified in the Spirit, seen of angels, preached unto the Gentiles, believed on in the world, received up into glory. (1 Tim. 3:16).
Except a man is pure in heart in all things, we are deceived. (Barnabas 12).	Unto the pure all things are pure; but unto them that are defiled and unbelieving is nothing pure: but even their mind and conscience is defiled. (Titus 1:15).
And if you have any remembrance of what is good, be mindful of me, meditating on these things, in order that both my desire and watchfulness may result in some good. (Barnabas 21, in closing).	Hold fast the form of sound words which thou hast heard of me, in faith and love which is in Christ Jesus. Watch thou in all things... for I am now ready to be offered, and the time of my departure is at hand. (2 Tim. 1:13 plus 4:5 a and 4:6

Beyond these parallels the Epistle of Barnabas rarely quotes from elsewhere in the New Testament. In these days before the four gospels were collected for regular possession and use the gospel of St. John was the version most used, being quoted by Ignatius, Polycarp and Papias, but the others are not yet much seen, apart from the St. Matthew with Ignatius at Antioch. Now the author of Barnabas appears to be using the Gospel according to St. Matthew, because the phrase "Many are called, but few chosen" given at the end of Barnabas 4 from Matthew 20:16 and 22:14 never appears elsewhere. Barnabas 4 is the Chapter concerned with formulating an escape from wickedness by realizing its dangers; beyond this Epistle it is a concern deeply general on the backcloth of Jesus' warning recorded in Mark 13 that tribulations and wars will continue until the end of the world age: there is no Divine enablement for us to clean it up into a sweet environment as an image of God's holy mountain where nothing hurts nor destroys (Isaiah 11:9). The need for the individual to stand against evil is ever present in a continuation of trial (without which we, in freewill to choose would have no point) where collective organization is necessarily part of the world in which it is only possible to form it. If the repentant and sincere believer walks back across time, so to speak, to put himself right at the foot of the cross, he may keep company spiritually with the likes of St. John. Here in Barnabas 4 and 6 the author has the two parts of Matthew 20:16 split: in Barn 6 "The Lord says, Behold, I will make the last like the first", which appears to be parallel with Paul in 2 Corinthians 5:17 "Any man in Christ is a new creature; old things are passed away. Behold, all things may become new". In Barnabas 5 "He came not to call the righteous, but sinners to repentance" is at Matthew 9:13b and also Mark 2:17 and Luke 5:32. It is probable however, that he took it from the Matthew. This use of the St. Matthew version in the Epistle points to either Antioch or Pontus-Bithynia, the two places being certainly connected with Simon Peter who greeted the latter in opening his own Epistle, an area to which Timothy could have been drawn through association with Barnabas and Mark – but this is only conjecture based on there being really no other candidates bringing the association together. Other than the few quotations outside of the Timothy parallels the Epistle contains by contrast some sixty amplified references back to the Old Testament. There is greater use of the ancient Scriptures in the Epistle of Barnabas, even though the work is of relatively late date, than in any of the New Testament books. Whatever his reason, the writer saw a contemporary need for this approach quite closely after St. John's time in Asia Minor; and either he knew nothing of John, or he avoided those parts holding the Johannine tradition; his project was aimed elsewhere toward men who had need of it, men considerably below the level of Ephesus and Smyrna. The project additionally looks back to Paul's kergyma noted in Acts 13:32-33 written in the sixties but spoken earlier, of the good tidings coming with Christ's sufferings under the purpose of God (as also with Simon Peter at Acts 2:23-24). However, in his own letters St. Paul does not discuss actually a scriptural warrant for Jesus' messiahship, sufferings and Resurrection. This may be due to the fact that, other than Rome, he was writing to Gentile communities who did not stand in need of clarification along Jewish lines. Paul had focused on such clarification in Romans 1:2-4, in Chapter 4, and in the Doctrine of Justification by Faith in Romans 8: there is certainly a probability that Jewish Christians comprised the community at Rome from the late thirties to its end in the mid-sixties. Now with the Epistle of Barnabas near the other end of this century there are signs in the project of an intention to accommodate the remaining Jewish Christian interests, which may still find a home in, again, Antioch and Pontus – an intent not unlike that of the St. Matthew author some thirty-five years earlier.

In general, little is definitely known about the second-century church communities. At Ephesus a broken-up large marble statue of Domitian has been found, probably of connection with a temple on the south-west edge of the city dedicated to the worship of that emperor in the late first century, which suggests a component uneasiness in the time of St. John there. At Smyrna in the first half of the second century, the period of St. Polycarp's ministry, the city itself followed a pagan imperial cult and contained many Jews who were hostile to the Christian faith. Although Ignatius (Ign. Smyrna 12:2) wrote in terms of a bishop and bodies of elders and deacons, it is possible that this was his advising to implement them – this method of community government might perhaps not yet be installed elsewhere than at Antioch, although as Timothy, appears to have been in Episcopal office and status in hte late sixties from first Timothy, he could be holding the office in Pontus, if we only knew. Fragments of second-century writing after about 125 give Christian leaders' names as bishops: Polycarp at his martyrdom and Papias at Hierapolis, a community which by Colossians 4:13 already existed in the early sixties but is not included in the Seven Letters to the Churches of Asia. According to Irenaeus writing much later, Papias Bishop of Hierapolis circa 120-140 was a colleague of Polycarp, but he does not seem to have known St. John personally. Papias was interested in collecting early authentic writings, and he probably used the Epistles First John and First Peter. He rather oddly preferred oral units to written books, and only fragments of his five-volume "Interpretation (or, Exposition) of the Lord's Oracles" of circa 135 survived to be used by Irenaeus and a few others later; but usefully he wrote some contemporary reference to important books. Besides the note of the Apostle Matthew having compiled a gospel of Sayings in the Hebrew, Papias recorded: "Mark, who became Peter's interpreter, wrote accurately, though not in order, all that he remembered of the things said and done by the Lord. For he had neither heard the Lord nor been one of His followers, but afterward, as I said, he had followed Peter, who used to compose his discourses with a view to the needs of his hearers, but not as if he were composing a systematic account of the Lord's sayings. So Mark did nothing blameworthy in thus writing some things just as he remembered them; for he was careful of this one thing, to omit none of the things he had heard and to state no untruth therein." Papias was quoting this from an unnamed elder, so it reflects what was currently believed in Asia Minor. Not many years later Justin Martyr ("Dialogue with Trypho the Jew") quoted material appearing only in St. Mark when he referred to "Peter's Memoirs": *Petron... en tois apomnhimoneumasin autou*, Peter... in these memoirs of his. In connection with Elders in the Region Papias also remarked, "Whenever a person came in my way who had attended on the Elders, I would enquire what were the declarations of the Elders, what was said by Andrew or Peter, or by Philip, Thomas or James, or by John, Matthew or by any other disciples of the Lord; and what Aristion and John the Elder, disciples of the Lord, say. For I did not think that I derived so much benefit from books as from the living voice of those that are still surviving". The presence here of two Johns has sometimes caused confusion, but the tense is split: St. John with the other Apostles clearly in the past, and another John among the Elders of Papias' present time whom he did know directly. There is no evidence or hint that Papias actually had contact with St. John the Apostle.

Other than Polycarp at Smyrna and Papias at Hierapolis there are no church specifics mentioned until at least 150. When in the 190's Polycrates Bishop of Ephesus called a synod of Asian bishops in connection with Victor Bishop of Rome's drive to fix a new date for Easter, he noted that the Apostle Philip had died at Hierapolis, also two aged virgin daughters of this Apostle there, and another daughter at Ephesus: so these women appear to have been there in the first quarter of the second century aged in their seventies plus and minus. Under Hadrian Iconium was made a Roman colony and Christianity continued there, an early Church Council being held there eventually in 235; at Sardis a bishop Melito is noted in the reign of Marcus Aurelius (161-180). The three communities at Colossae, Hierapolis and Laodicea had joint religious development (vide Colossians 2:1 and 4: 13-16) in St. Paul's time, but by the fourth century Laodicea became the most prominent bishopric in this area. Although belonging originally to Asia Minor Irenaeus went, like Marcion, to the west, and is only known as a bishop at Lyons in Gaul, which is France.

In the first half of the second century the position regarding a canon of books formed together as the New Testament seems to have been, that while a considerable amount of oral tradition was still functioning as the accepted method of transmission the use of written books was slow in coming. St. Paul's letters had been collected near the end of the first century, and Clement of Rome may have been a main instrument in adding Romans as the most difficult of access. Of the seven Catholic Epistles in the canon only First John and First Peter were used as yet, and strangely as it seems, the Pastoral Epistles were apparently not known in Western Asia Minor during this period – perhaps simply because Timothy had not seen reason to publish them, which is reasonable. Very likely an inclination arose, to form the canon as a collection of the four gospels with Paul's letters and two Catholic Epistles, as a reaction to what Marcion had done at Rome in first, but misguided, effort at it. It is unclear when Acts of Apostles was included, and all other books were certainly added later. If the hypothesis of the basic idea of coupling the gospels with apostolic authority for an equipment distinct from the old Jewish canon had started with Marcion is true, then this dates the early drive for the New Testament to the period 130-150: at the end of our century under review, that since the glorious Resurrection. It seems a very long time taken to have got there; but we cannot judge the first and second centuries by ideas of the twenty-first. The believing communities were small and widely scattered, and communication was slow in those days. Further, the making of book copies was a very slow and labourious process. When Simon Peter and Barnabas desired that the knowledge should be set in a permanent and written form and so Mark carried it out, they could scarcely imagine it would be some seventy-five years future to the St. Mark project before such gospel records, of the utmost value, would be brought into use; but no doubt the almost universal illiteracy was a heavy retarding factor. But once the collection had been made – in an era when numerous spurious books were being written – it provided immensely useful and effective equipment in the ongoing struggle against heresies. For all its lateness, the canon was certainly timely of arrival in that regard.

Of the gospels themselves, only that of John is definitely known of the place of writing, as Ephesus. With the others Matthew is likely to have been done at Antioch, Luke possibly in his home patch of Macedonia, and Mark at either Ephesus or Troas. There is little doubt that the Birth and Infancy narratives were added to the St. Luke gospel in a clumsy way; this portion may have originally opened the St. Mark gospel and if so, then it was broken off the Mark scroll by the time (from 64 and requested by Barnabas and Luke in the following year) Luke had access to it. In his own gospel Luke (3:2) introduces John the Baptist as the son of Zacharias and Jesus by means of a long genealogy through Joseph, which is superfluous to the detailed account of their origin. If the material presented as Luke 1 and 2 was added to Luke before either of these gospels was much copied, it must have been done at the place where the detached portion of Mark was first received together with the gospel of Luke, possibly Philippi which is not far from Ephesus and Troas. When the St. Mark gospel was later used as a major source by the St. Matthew author it would very likely be a copy made from the same broken scroll used by Luke.

Taking it all round, this century from 33 to the 130's was a period not entirely satisfactory from the Christian progress point of view. The believer might hope and expect, but there are natural factors accounting for this. The first generation (thirties to the mid-sixties) were not in doubt, since these people were at first hand with the action; but thereafter the progress of the Christian torch must depend upon the persuasive strength and quality of the witnessing and teaching, which although safe in the hands of John, Mark and Luke beyond the days of Paul, Simon Peter and Barnabas, had probably less guarantee to continue in the time approaching the 130's when only Polycarp is known with full certainly as an equivalent luminary. The communities were geographically isolated as yet, and probably not much in touch. Another factor retarding the progress of this faith system was the continual struggle the Christians had to undergo against pagan, Jewish and heretical oppositions which must surely sap the energy of the communities and their luminaries away from the main work of developing an inherent strength to manifest a perpetuation of the early Pi, instead of seeing it fade considerably and inexorably down the decades: they were not free to grow as they might in normal unimpeded circumstances. Indeed, there is much to be thankful for in the fact that by such fine efforts as they did make, the Christian faith following did not die either at individual level or as an organized Church institution. The Christian torch may have been extinguished in Jewish hands, but not in Gentile. It behoves us now in far distant modern (or, post-modern some say) times to take the torch again from the hands of the early second century in a sense, and put overall matters right by seizing it in our freedom from most of those old retarding factors, added to our enormous communication advantages, and making good the early unavoidable deficiency. If the believer successfully resists reduction in the fight against evil he may continue to fight in other days; but he who once succumbs to the invisible evil influence at any time, is finished.

11
Epilogue

Although later matters are beyond this first century 33 to the 130's, it is useful to glance further at the still early outcome for Christianity as a whole, in that the overall picture has, in a large sense, involved failure.

In this the Christian historian might work back from the answer, so to speak, taking the 312 conversion of Constantine as the late limit time point. The second and third centuries era was a time of wide confusion in the secular with a popular hobby of myth-making, but then also an era in which people would be hungering for truth as indeed the Greeks did in the first century days of St. Paul. By the turn of the third to fourth century the Roman society had suffered continuous and deep decadence. The reaction of emperors to the developed Christianity expressing in the world its comprehensive fellowship of unity under uncompromising leadership, differed: Decius (249-251), Valerian (253-259) and Diocletian (302-312) all made persecuting thrusts against the Christians, the last of these in deepest desperation, whereas Constantine joined them immediately on emerging from the ruck, because he could see familiarities of power in the church as a potential capability to provide imperial solutions for those reduced times. Possibly it was across the third century that Christianity, such as it was, became a force to be reckoned with; for the earlier local persecutions were only briefly accounted in pagan popular connection, not broadly and official in the Roman

State as were those later: the second half of the third century emerges as a period of new concerns.

Historically and in the secular the third century was a dreary period, even in India of the Sakas and the Kushans between the Mauryan and Gupta empires, and here of Caesars known as the Barrack Emperors who owed their election to the military, eighteen emperors between Severus and Diocletian. Generally the Christians in the Roman Raj were insulated from those rulers by the administrative problems with which each of the short-lived reigns had to deal, but in this comparative freedom Church leaders were engaging in monarchical stresses of their own. Such men as Victor Bishop of Rome (202), Stephen (258), Dionysius (268), Cyprian (martyred in 258), Clement of Alexandria (died in 220) and Tertullian (died after 220) were interested in making themselves manifest as powerful ecclesiastics; but there were exceptions to this among the contemporary Christian salient figures: St. Gregory Thaumaturgus, a pupil of Origen born of pagan parents and consecrated as a bishop in 238, who was reputed to be a miracle-worker and whose flock of believers steadily increased during the mid-century persecutions, and Origen himself who, as essentially a lay writer, was denied canonization by the later Church. According to the fourth century historian Eusebius "The evil spirit aimed at Origen his deadliest violence", although when Origen had to flee from his hometown of Alexandria in 215 when the emperor Caracalla set out to massace the learned, he was given refuge at Caesarea in the protection of its bishop and also of the Bishop of Jerusalem. Eventually at Tyre in the Decian persecution he was tortured and died there in 253 at the age of 67, in reality a martyr unrecognized as such. Origen suffered throughout most of his life; but the saint is proved by tribulation. Perhaps it is true that this man who sought to anchor Christians in the Scriptures by education, was the deepest thinker since the Apostles; but there was already conflict within the Church as well as outside it.

By the end of the second century the churches at Rome and Carthage, the churches of the West, were well established. There were seventy bishops in North Africa by 225, about the time Quintus Septimus Florens Teretullian died after initiating ecclesiastical Latin. Born in about 155 Tertullian came fairly late in life to Christianity in his thirties (circa 190), being impressed by the strength of martyrs and with uncomprising vigour generally, but it is not known whether he was ever ordained as a priest, being known principally as a writer. Shortly before 210 Tertullian left the Orthodox Church to join a new sectarian movement of Montanism (founded by a Phyrgian prophet Montanus) which had spread from Asia Minor to North Africa; it is probable that he had become dissatisfied with a current laxity among Christians. He then became the movement's most articulate spokesman for these who opposed any compromise with the ways of the world – believing the end of the world to be imminent – in combination with their stringent and demanding moralism. But this was, as what we would now term a splinter group, outside the mainstream of the Church, and it was as a moralist holding the view that Christianity must stand totally against its surrounding culture, rather than as a philosopher, that he asked "What has Athens to do with Jerusalem?"

What of the Roman Church of the West, from which Tertullian withdrew himself? A new Christian community was founded in this city shortly after the accession of Hadrian when it became again possible. Apart from the virtual impossibility of such in the time of the Flavian emperors it seems certain that when Trajan desired to discover what the Christian gatherings might entail, he sent for a survey thus to be made to a governor in a district a thousand miles distant. This could hardly be necessary if there was a community in Rome. Perhaps the earliest known name at Rome is Marcion, who came from Pontus on the Black Sea in about the mid-thirties of the second century to a community founded in about 125 contemporary with Hadrian's rebuilding of Jerusalem as Aelia Capitolina where Christians were permitted to be but Jews excluded. As son of a bishop (of Sinope) Marcion came from an orthodox background and might have been a pillar of the Church; but he was influenced by Gnostic heretical ideas (without himself becoming an adherent of that heresy) which veered him away from the orthodoxy of Old Testament acceptance. He has the honour of forming a first known canon of New Testament books, but it was distorted down to inclusion of only the gospel of Luke and the Pauline Epistles (with Jew components removed from Galatians and Romans), and he broke with the Roman Church in 144. Anecitus as Bishop of Rome in about 150 requested Polycarp Bishop of Smyrna to agree on a proposal to adjust the date for celebration of Easter from the then held Quartodeciman adoption of the Jewish fourteenth of Nisan to a Roman practice of taking the next Lord's Day after it.

This was not agreed, matters were left as they stood, but it marks the beginning of the Easter Controversy. Some forty years later Victor, who seems to have been the second Bishop of Rome, threatened an excommunication with the Eastern bishops who refused to conform as he renewed the demand for a change from the Quartodeciman practice which had undoubtedly been in use from the times of the Apostles. It seems to have been motivated by some desire to distance the Roman Church from all Jewish antecedents where possible, perhaps originally influenced by Marcion. As a close connection between Asia Minor and Gaul existed in the second century, Polycarp's disciple Irenaeus as thereby become Bishop of Lyon in the far West (succeeding Pothinus from the martyrdoms in persecution there in 177) was able to mediate in this Easter dispute where he considered Church unity to be of greater importance than festival dates. He did not accept Marcionite ideas, but may have been inspired here from the general fact that our Lord Himself was less concerned with outward conformity to legal regulations than with the spirit of their observance. In any event John 19:13 shows the crucifixion day of the week to have been a Thursday (Jewish Sabbath beginning on Friday afternoon thence to Saturday evening) when by Luke 23:54 "the Sabbath drew on" in the evening of burial unto the scriptural three nights in the tomb – not two. It poses a question as to how far some of the Churchmen laying down law for others to conform, knew their subject?

The Church, at least in the West, was already capable of schismatic tendency by the time Tertullian opted for uncompromising Montanism. The young Roman Church of as yet only three quarters of a century had in her earliest days as Gentile (the community here was of Jews in the former time of St. Paul) carried along the unorthodox Marcion who thought in terms of the Creator in the Old Testament as a God separate from the Father of Jesus; it is not certain whether he left the Church of his own accord, or was expelled. Nor is it easy to conjecture how the phenomenon of Roman ecclesiastical aggrandizement originated. However, this phenomenon made use of an important principle held by Irenaeus, viz. that Episcopal office provided the only safe guide in interpreting the Scriptures, on which a contemporary attempt in the late second century was made to draw up a list of bishops by which to establish succession from the Apostles; they were thinking along descendant lines, assuming direct succession might be demonstrated. Certainly the bishops form an organized body of college: it is an Episcopal succession. But Roman ideas of their particular pontiff as successor to Simon Peter goes unacceptably beyond collegial succession – in particular, that apostolic claim is not grounded in proven historical fact of Simon ever having been in Rome even if the extension beyond the college could be right in principle. Was the Bishop of Rome regarded as first among the bishops merely in that Rome was the imperial capital? Such regard is not upheld from the heavy fight against the principal danger of Gnosticism being fought elsewhere, nor did Constantine retain Rome as his Christian capital, but set up a new capital without delay a thousand miles eastward. The political-looking aspects of episcopacy developed from mid-second to late third century, by which time the Church was ready to marry the world. But by about 150 she had lost the Presbyterian democracy of Corinth and Ephesus in which the educating power of the faith spread horizontally among the "peculiar people of royal priesthood... able to give reason for the hope that is in them", which if achieved in onward development must, with automatic forbearance and comprised of families praying together and staying together, have produced a society of people possessed of spiritual light and heat. There is no vertical prominence of figureheads in the holy gospel.

This aspect of an educating power was not ignored in the period of these two centuries; the literature of faith enablement inherited from Paul, Mark, the Hebrews author and John, stood in a further literary way behind certain men in the next century and a half. Whereas many bishops were merely powerful ecclesiastics – among whom Cyprian of Carthage seems to represent the beginning of the papal Petrine succession idea, there were men of a very different stamp in the second century closer to the original Christian ashram not only in time but also in truth. In this era the Christian activities and its greatest men were certainly centred upon Asia Minor where Polycarp, the only known case of direct apostolic succession (from St. John) appears to have led a blameless life. A little later his pupil Irenaeus was fully occupied with the contemporary struggle against the Gnostic heresy in its varied forms, and his five-volume Adversus haeresses "Against Heretics" was written in about 180 to refute the Gnosticsm of spirit good/matter evil ideas which tried to fit Christ into a hotch-potch of pre-Christian Eastern beliefs, as a non-preexisting subordinate agent, on a charlatanic basis that they had in this a special secret knowledge (hence the appellation from gnowsis, "knowledge"). It had begun in St. John's time, and was not soon smashed; for from a background of Roman gods, emperor-worship, polytheistic mystery religions and Greek Hermeticism, a tendency for heresies to develop among the ignorant was practically inevitable. John had met the early Gnostics by writing his gospel account in which the truth of Jesus is shown from first hand with the utmost clarity: but almost a century later Irenaeus, with his hands as full as ever against them, had not the luxury of writing as an educator but only as a representative enemy of error. He had served as an arbiter in churches of Asia Minor after about 150 and before moving westward to Lyon in Gaul – the furthest extremity west in contemporary Christendom – and he seems to have contributed to the development of Episcopal official authority which was to "take off" in the next century. Some claim might be made for him towards the field of religious education in that he was further instrumental in more greatly establishing the creed and in drawing together which must have had widening effect, although after Polycarp's time the flock tended to be left outside by men who veered towards a fuller occupation with the battles among themselves, even before the swathe of this in the fourth century. As an early Christian writer Irenaeus reflected still earlier tradition when he wrote: "For Adam had necessarily to be restored in Christ, that mortality be absorbed in immortality; and Eve in Mary that a virgin, as become the advocate of a virgin, should undo and destroy virginal disobedience by virginal obedience". Here the fifteenth of First Corinthians is visible, but the traditional unit may antedate even that. How was it that the blasphemous "queen of heaven" Theotokus idea emerged later?

Of the writers who functioned outside the pale of the struggling bishops, Justin Martyr c. 100-165 was perhaps the earliest well known, although there was earlier writing in apologetics. His philosopher-apologist work shows the first positive encounter of Christian revelation with Greek philosophy after he had become a Christian in 132 at either Ephesus or Smyrna. After 135 Justin worked as an itinerant preacher to pagans, and in 150 he wrote his Major Apology which defended the Christians against charges of atheism and hostility to the Roman State, a defence which he addressed to Antininus Pius and the son-in-law Marcus Aurelius expressing the core of his Christian philosophy: "The highest aspiration of both

Christianity and Platonic philosophy is a transcendent and unchangeable God. Consequently an intellectual articulation of the Christian faith will demonstrate its harmony with reason. Such a convergence is rooted in the relationship between human reason and the Divine mind, both identified with the same term logos" world of time, creation, freedom, the human soul's affinity with the Divine Spirit, and the recognition of good and evil". This was a magnificent attempt, but the imperial recipients may have realized that faith transcends reason: that it is unwise to attempt the impossible. They are not recorded to have said, as did Agrippa to Paul, "Almost you persuade us to be Christian. Justin followed the Johannine logos theology with intention to follow in Christ's steps by teaching His basic and comprehensive truths so as to save men from the power of evil, during which activity he described only two sacraments: eucharist and baptism. He mentions the first three gospels and quotes from Hebrews, the Epistles of Paul, First Peter and perhaps from Acts of Apostles, but this last is uncertain. In another work, *Dialogue with Trypho: The Jew* Justin tried to demonstrate that a new covenant has superseded the old covenant with the Hebrews: that Jesus is both Messiah and the pre-existing logos through Whom God revealed Himself in the scriptures of classical prophet inspirations, and that the Gentile nations now replaced the ancients in the Divine choosing. Further, in a short Second Apology he argued that Roman persecution of Christians was unjust; however, no such persecution in contemporary time is known of other than the pagan-driven purge at Lyon in 177 which was posthumous to Justin martyred in Rome when, after debating with a cynic Crescens he was denounced to the Roman Prefect as a subversive and condemned to death in 165.

Other apologists were busy in the second century not only towards Roman authorities but also against all comers in opposition such as Galen of Pergamum (129-c199) and the middle Platonist thinker Celsus, who flourished in the 170's. It was necessary for Christianity to define its position as well as defend it in relation to the Hellenistic culture, in effect to defend the innocent flock of its believers albeit indirectly, against the intellectual rabble. The earlier apologist Quadratus addressed an apology to Hadrian in 124, outlining the Christian faith, and similarly such was addressed by Aristides in about 140 to Antininus Pius. In later years Athenagoras' Embassy for the Christians and his On the Resurrection of the Dead were not unfriendly to the Greek cultural philosophy; but all these works of an educational character refuted spurious charges against Christians and strove to vindicate the Christian understanding of God and of specific doctrines such as the divinity of Christ and the resurrection of the body. In a sense these writers were the first Christian theologians out in the world. The next logical layer of luminaries after the Apostles. But it was Justin's pupil Tatian, a man who saw only evil in the Graeco-Roman civilization and sharply attacked paganism, who came closest to directly outreaching to the wide Christian flock when in about 172 he assembled the gospel accounts as a single unit by writing them up as his Diatessaron, literally "Across Four Together"; this was after he had broken with the Roman Church and returned home to Syria. Tatian rejected the classical literary and moral values of the Greeks as corrupt, and repudiated their intellectualism as he embraced the synthesis of Christian monotheism with the Stoic concept of an intermediary logos creating the rational and purposeful cohesion of the universe. By this he wrote also a discourse to the Greeks. An action of collection the gospel accounts in one, removing material of repeating, and arranging the material chronologically as well as doctrinally is a remarkably good and educational exercise, but it requires a foundation of already long writing experience to properly back such undertaking.

In the late second century general philosophy leaned towards religious mysticism and, apart from the general Gnostic problem, a Neoplatonist school at Alexandria fought bitterly against Christianity. Christian thought deepened and its theology developed in reaction against this, and here began the age of Origen of Alexandria, Oregenes Adamantus the last of the pukka Christians to be for a very long time. Some twenty years before Origen was born the pagan writer Celsus had written the first serious criticism of Christianity in Alethes logos "The True Doctrine" which seems not to have found reaction by Christian contemporaries such as for instance Irenaeus; but it is easily possible that this bishop knew nothing of it, having moved away to the far West near to that time. Also, he was preoccupied with inner tensions within the Church, not with external pagan views. According to Celsus, "If all men wanted to be Christians, the Christians would no longer want them." No doubt he was writing in ignorance of his subject, as he brusquely dismissed Christianity as a crude and bucolic onslaught on the religious traditions and intellectual values of classical culture: "The Christian miracles are insufficiently attested and most improbable. But even if genuine they could hardly offset the miracles of the (pagan) world." This claim is possibly a referring to Asclepius the patron-hero of ancient Greek medicine who – if he existed – is supposed to have been killed with a thunderbolt from the mythical god Zeus... Yet it was some seventy years before this pagan critical rubbish came to be refuted at length by Origen at the request of one of his converts Ambrose, who materially supported him. In the paragraph-by-paragraph satisfactory vindication of Christianity against pagan attack which Origen's Contra Celsus achieved, he claimed in his sustained rejoinder that a philosophical mind has a right to think within the Christian framework, and that this faith system is neither a prejudice of unreasoning masses nor a prop for social outcasts.

Contra Celsus was written near the end of Origen's life, an ascetic life in which he had suffered much since his teen years. This man had already done a good deal of writing as a teacher, theologian and Bible-scholar, notably in Hexapla the synopsis of six Old Testament versions, and his thirty-two volume commentary on St. John which was undertaken in defence against a heretic Heracleon. He face ecclesiastical hatred – something which ought not to exist – and hostile gossip; and although highly orthodox in devotion to the cause of the Christian faith with a lasting influence, he was posthumously denounced by smaller men, often misquoted perhaps deliberately, and a long edict of Justinian in 543 denouncing Origen as a heretic was extended by bishops at the Ecumenical Council of Constantinople in 553. They wrongly supposed that this, the greatest Christian teacher after the Apostles, was pretending the Son to be inferior to the Father (precursing the Arian heresy 315-370 against which Athanasius alone fought the Church for fifty years) and that he denied hell (the basis of their religion of fear). Again, this kind of thing is necessarily born of ignorance. Before 231 Origen had written his De principiis "On First Principles", a large and ordered statement of Christian doctrine in which every Christian is committed to the rule of faith laid down by the Apostles. It upholds the Creator as God of both Old and New Testaments, the incarnation of the pre-existent Lord, the Holy Spirit as One of the Divine Triad, the freedom of rational souls, the existence of discarnate (i.e. invisible) spirits, the temporal limitation of the world, and judgment to come.

The condemnation of this man was unjustifiable, but it reflects the common way of the world. Probably the Church machinery chose to discount Origen as his being simply a lay-writing and lay-teaching outsider in a familiar world where it is not what you did, but who you were when you did it. The essence of this bright flash in the post-first century pan is this: In continual emphasis upon spiritual apprehension and a theology ultimately turning upon the goodness of God and the creature in freewill for the proving, the highest prayer is an elevation of the soul beyond material things to a passive inward union with Christ the Mediator between men and the Father (vide Hebrews). The transcendent God is the source of all existence: good, just and omnipotent Who, in overflowing love created rational spiritual beings through the Logos (vide St. John), an act involving a degree of self-limitation on God's part.

As one giving the greatest single impulse to the development of Christian theology between the times of St. John and Augustine (Early fifth century) Origen believed the material world to be a discipline for trial and proving: "If you remove freewill from virtue, you destroy its essence", also in the pre-existence of souls but not in transmigration nor any rational souls into animal bodies. Further, that redemption restores all souls to their original blessed state, and none are wholly beyond it; where God punishes, the punishment is remedial. The union of God and man in Christ is the pattern for that further union of Christ and the believer, thus redemption restores fallen souls from matter to spirit, from image to reality. He thought hell to be not an absolute, since God will not abandon any creature, and God's love will ultimately triumph; and was convinced that Christ's work remains unfinished until He has subdued all unto Himself. It is not good to ask or answer "if" or "what if" questions nor sensible to dwell on what might have been. Yet even so, one can summarize in saying that the second-century straight apologists though very well intending did not manage to bring any of its three possible emperors Hadrian, Antonius Pius and particularly Marcus Aurelius into this faith system, while in the third century the Big Boss complex was forced forward. By the time they did get a nominally Christian emperor early fourth century, the damage was done.

Appendix Note – Mystery

And without controversy great is the mystery of godliness. God was manifest in the flesh, justified in the Spirit, seen of angels, preached unto the Gentiles, believed on in the world, received up into glory". – First Timothy 3:16.

Perhaps originally musterion derives from a meaning "closed from the eyes"; in the Hebrew m'str's is "hidden, secret things", and it is possible that the Greeks adopted it firstly applicable as of "religious secret", more so than as used in the Hebrew. The term is used in religious senses exclusively in Greek writings, especially the New Testament. Indeed, the whole Gospel is the revealing of an open secret. By Mark 4:11 divine revelation is firstly bestowed on closest faith: "Unto you (i.e. already in faith") it is given to know the mystery of the kingdom of God; but unto them that are without, all things are done in parables. "Generally in the scriptural use of the term a mystery signifies a unit or point in the field of Religion of which one can know nothing except by revelation, and nothing more than is revealed. It is essential to realize that any knowledge from revelation is received by faith only; it can be used as a principle in human reasoning's, but must not itself be disputed as if it were itself open to human argument. At Mark 4:24-25 subjectively from 4:11 the text shows that any one of God's special gifts is an earnest of others, that as with the tiny seed symbolic of a start towards heaven (vide Mark 4:30-32) a possessing of some faith through grace can, by that grace, receive more in due time. A reversal is implied where a lack through falling away must result in deprivation of attainments and advantages in which the unfaithful holder had trusted and gloried – it is necessary to get the priorities right. The process of revelation by divine grace divulging a religious mystery is most clearly written in the fourth of Mark, where the ministry of Jesus is identified with the kingdom of God; and in the detail of the writing of these particular units there was historically close association, Mark writing in about the year 64 and his uncle Barnabas writing to his protégé Timothy in about 67. In the St. Thomas Gospel of Sayings the whole work is presented as a direct disclosure from heaven, in illuminating a former mysterious darkness by the newly supplied path of light; and it is easy to see how communities of confused little men might take it up in a totally erroneous direction, as the Gnostics did, through no fault or intention of the original writer. To Paul, writing in the intervening years between Thomas and Mark, the term "mystery" only seems to have embraced the idea of Gentile and Jewish differencing (Romans 11:25f with 9:1-4 and 16:25-26). With him the blindness of the Jews was a deeply felt concern. His text at Colossians 1:23-27 written at Rome in about 61 suggests an associating with Barnabas at that time, and his phrase of the mystery "now is made manifest to His saints" is close to the position of his co-worker writing Ephesians 3:9-10 where the mystery manifest institutionally in the body of the church (see also Ephesians 5:31-32). In other texts such as Revelation 1:20 the term really means "symbol".

In the secular sense a mystery is taken to be a denoting of something hard to understand, either as intrinsically obscure or as transcending reason – which in fact faith does. Human freedom in freewill to harmonise with the Divine Omnipotence exemplifies such. But in the scriptural a mystery is a unit of importance to be disclosed, God the Father's dispensations to some extent made known. It rises far above St. Paul's "The truth of the calling of the Gentiles to an equal place with Jews in the family of God was a mystery hidden from ages and from generations" because, if we read the gospel in real depth towards more fully realizing what it means, it is possible to realize application to all of mankind since Adam. The ancient Hebrews were different only in that they chose monotheism and therefore the inspired classical prophetic writings were vouchsafed to them – nothing else, and they had no business to be writing a large body of fiction in which to perpetually believe. At 1 Timothy 3:16 Barnabas summarized what had controversially been a mystery but had been subsequently revealed, certainly believed by the writer of the Egyptian Gospel, but several decades were to pass before men generally would codify it in the way later expressed.

Index

A

Acts of Apostles 1, 29, 100-101, 127, 175, 185

Agrippa (Herod Agrippa) 19, 75, 185

Alexandria 35, 83, 128, 179, 186-187

Antioch in Pisidia 37, 40, 63, 67

Antioch in Syria 33-35, 40, 44, 63, 79, 81, 101, 105, 151

Apocalypse of St. John 122

Apollos 60, 81-83, 128-129

Apostles, collectively 27, 30-31, 61, 103

Aquila and Priscilla 67, 81, 108

Athens 44, 66-67, 69, 70

B

Baptism, baptizing 29, 37, 81, 185

Barnabas, St. 11, 32-38, 48,-51,, 85, 99, 101, 104, 106, 108

Barnabas, Epistle of, 163, 165, 167, 170, 172

Believers 16, 18, 22, 25, 34, 64, 110, 121

Berea 66

Birth Narrative, critical points upon 100-101, 136-137, 175

Bithynia 64, 67, 80, 154-155, 165, 171

C

Chain of graces 94

Christian, appellation as 33

Christian – Jew split 79, 115, 130, 138, 158, 166

Church 2, 27, 31, 60, 80, 93, 105, 110, 111, 126, 138, 183

Claudius, emperor 20, 39, 67, 82, 96, 117

Clement of Rome 86, 148-149, 174

Colossae 60, 98, 113-115, 121, 174

Conversion of Saul 16, 43

Corinth 35, 47, 49, 55-59, 64, 67, 69-70, 82-84

Corinthan Letters 48, 56-58, 71

Crete 104,105, 129

Cultural Shock 42, 68, 142

Cyprus 35, 36, 85

D

Damascus 16, 32, 34, 43

Dates of:
Apollos arrival at Ephesus 83

Barnabas and Saul on first tour 34

Birth of St. Paul, 71

Birth of St. Peter 78

Christ's passion and Resurrection 90, 122

Conference on circumcision 34, 48

Death of St. Paul 103

Epistle of James 86

Epistle to Philippians 99

Epistle of Simon Peter 91

John, St. to Ephesus 118

Judaisers visit to Antioch 41

Luke's Book of Acts. 108

Luke's departure from Rome 100

Mark, St. gospel project 101.

Martyrdom of James 87-88

Martyrdom of Stephen 31

Murder of James Zebedee 77

Naming of Baranbas 30

Pastroral Epistles 103

Arrival at Corinth 67

Arrival at Troas 69

Departure from Corinth 70.

Final arrival at Jerusalem 73

Paul's Letters 48

Paul's rejection and return to Tarsus 32

Derbe 39-40, 63-68

Domitian, Emperor 137, 148-151, 154

E

Egyptian Gospel of Thomas 2-3, 11-13, 18, 30, 138, 192

Epahras 60, 98, 105, 134

Epistles written at Rome 48, 55, 99, 103

Essence of Paul's Letter 54, 57

Essence of St. John 146-148

Euphoria, post-Resurrection 14, 17, 92, 102, 3

Evidence of the Resurrection 17, 19, 24

F

Felix and Festus 73-74, 117

Fire in Rome 98, 103

G

Galatians 18, 28, 32, 34, 36, 41, 44, 47-48, 51-53, 55, 61, 64, 77, 79, 85, 181

Gallio 70, 97

Gamaliel 138, 150

Gentiles 12, 29, 32, 35, 37-39, 49

Gospels, writing of, 17

H

Hadrian, emperor, 163-164, 180, 186, 189

Hebrews, author of 12, 128-129-131, 183

Hegesippus 87-88, 115, 154

Hellenistic 19, 35, 61

Heresies 114, 145, 151, 153, 175, 183

Historical Significance 25

Holy Spirit 32, 50, 70, 75, 121, 158, 188

I

Iconium 39, 63, 174

Ignatius, St. 80, 86, 138, 154, 155-156, 160, 164

Individual aspect 23-24, 76, 106

J

James of Jerusalem 28, 41, 51, 77, 86-88, 100, 103, 108

Jerusalem 28, 32-36, 53, 73, 84, 114, 118, 139, 148

Jewish opposition 38-39

John, St. 12-13, 26-27, 100, 108, 115, 118, 121, 137, 140, 143, 151-152,

John as writer 142-143

Josephus 28, 87, 135-136

Judaizers 41, 50-53, 105, 113, 152

Jude, St 114, 115, 128

Justification by Faith, doctrine of 38, 58, 172

Justin Martyr 118, 158, 173, 184-185

K

Kingdom of heaven 4, 9, 60, 133

L

Letter of Clement 149-151

Letter of Pilate to Claudius 21,

Letter of Pliny the younger 154-155

Luke, St. 26, 47, 64-65, 111, 134

Luke as a writer 29, 34, 62, 64, 67, 75, 100, 134,136

Luke's gospel 26, 127, 137

Luke's prefaces 75, 100

Lystra 37, 39, 63, 68, 83

M

Marcion 101, 148, 161-162, 164-165, 174-175, 180-182

Mark, St. 35-37, 42, 80, 111

Mark as a writer 102-103

Mark's gospel 16-17, 20, 45, 61, 102-103, 127, 131, 134

Matthew gospel 79, 80

Messianic Texts 31, 51

Miletus 73, 108

N

Nazarins 15, 30, 34, 34, 113

Nero, emperor 96, 98, 103, 108

New Testament canon 174-176

O

Objections in Pauline ascriptions 54

Office of bishop 80

Old Testament texts, use of, 47, 165

Overall lesson from Simon Peter 95

P

Pagans 39, 43, 117, 119, 144, 153, 184

Papias 138, 173, 174

Parallels: Epistles James and Peter 95

Pastorals and Epistle of Barnabas 163, 165, 167, 172, 175

Pastorals and Ephesians 110-111

Pastoral Epistles 85, 103, 105, 110-111, 127, 160, 163, 167, 175

Patmos 115, 118-119, 152

Index

Paul, St. side reference to 16, 24, 36-37, 42, 44-45, 47-48, 53, 61

Pharisees 15, 20, 139

Philip the Apostle 28, 174

Philippi 60, 73, 83, 99

Philippians 60, 84, 97, 99, 100

Polycarp 140, 144, 154, 156, 158-160

Proselytes 43, 93, 150

R

Romans, Epistle to the 47, 58, 71, 84

Rome 47, 58, 71, 84, 108, 149

S

Sadducees 19, 139

Samaria, Samaritans, 28, 77, 116-117, 118, 142

Saul of Tarsus 15, 28, 31, 32

Second Coming of Christ, assumed 54, 102, 130

Seneca 96

Sermon on the Mount, circumstance of, 115

Seven Letters to Asia 114, 119, 122, 127, 173

Simon Peter, 14, 27-30, 32, 40, 51, 77-79, 158

Simon Peter, Epistle of 86, 90, 114-115,

Simon Peter, name of 92-93

Smyrna 156, 158, 160, 162, 172, 174, 181, 184

Stephen, St. 2, 16, 19, 28, 31, 43, 45, 179

Stoics, Stoicism 43, 121

T

Tarsus 34, 35, 43, 44, 45

Theological 22, 55, 66, 123

Thessalonika 84, 105, 122

Thomas, St. 11, 12-13, 14, 28, 30, 118

Timotheus 63, 64, 66, 81, 83-84

Timothy, St. 60, 63-64, 85, 105, 108, 111, 129, 171

Titus 48, 64, 81, 84, 103-104, 105, 108, 129

Trajan, emperor 140, 155

Troas 69, 73, 108, 175

V

Vespasian, emperor 117, 119, 148, 154, 197

W

Witness, specific 30, 50, 63, 99

Women at the Cross 87

www.ingramcontent.com/pod-product-compliance
Lightning Source LLC
Chambersburg PA
CBHW032043150426
43194CB00006B/398